At David C Cook, we equip the local church around the corner and around the globe to make disciples. Come see how we are working together—go to **www.davidccook.com**. Thank you!

transforming lives together

I'D LIKE YOU MORE
IF YOU WERE
MORE LIKE ME

LEADER CONNECT GUIDE

I'D LIKE YOU MORE IF YOU WERE MORE LIKE ME

GETTING REAL ABOUT GETTING CLOSE

LEADER CONNECT GUIDE

JOHN ORTBERG

WITH LAURA DERICO

David C Cook

transforming lives together

I'D LIKE YOU MORE IF YOU WERE MORE LIKE ME
LEADER CONNECT GUIDE
Published by David C Cook
4050 Lee Vance Drive
Colorado Springs, CO 80918 U.S.A.

David C Cook U.K., Kingsway Communications
Eastbourne, East Sussex BN23 6NT, England

The graphic circle C logo is a registered trademark of David C Cook.

ISBN 978-1-4347-1192-2
eISBN 978-1-4347-1259-2

Material in this resource is adapted from:
I'd Like You More if You Were More like Me: Getting Real about Getting Close.
Copyright © 2017 by John Ortberg.
Published by Tyndale Momentum, Carol Stream, Illinois 60188. Used by permission.

Related titles:
I'd Like You More if You Were More like Me Member Connect Guide
I'd Like You More if You Were More like Me DVD
I'd Like You More if You Were More like Me Small Group Connection Kit
I'd Like You More if You Were More like Me Church Connection Kit

All epigraphs and feature quotes within this book, unless otherwise
noted, are excerpted from *I'd Like You More if You Were More like
Me: Getting Real about Getting Close*, by John Ortberg.

The Team: Laura Derico, JamieLyn Heim, Toben Heim,
Verne Kenney, Nick Lee, Wendi Lord, Dave Thornton
Cover Design: Nick Lee with Jacqueline L. Nuñez
Cover Photo: Shutterstock/Ermolaev Alexander
Printed in the United States of America

2 3 4 5 6 7 8 9 10 11

111517

CONTENTS

INTRODUCTION

USING THE I-WORD AND OTHER TIPS

Welcome! This is a study about getting close to one another. It's about developing the kind of relationships that challenge us, sharpen us, support us, and grow us. It's about building the kind of relationships that God wants us to have with others and that he wants to have with us.

Whether this is your first time working through a small group study or your thirty-first time, you are sure to have some new experiences here. Some of those experiences will make you feel right at home. And that's a good thing. Some of those experiences may make you feel a little uncomfortable. That's good too.

Look at the cover of the book you are holding. Notice the word *Leader*? That's you, friend. That means it's your job to lead a group of people through the study material we've provided for you. Don't worry—it's great stuff, so you're in good hands! But just to put you a little more at ease, let's take a look at a session together.

Every time you meet with your group, you'll spend some time getting to know one another and getting to know the subject of the particular session through discussion and group exercises. Check out the Session Menu to get an idea of what to expect.

SESSION MENU

In Group

    Open Up: eat, watch video, talk, pray

    Connect: discuss, do exercises

    Bible Connect: group Bible study

    Go Out: pray and go

Out of Group

    Pray, do exercises, think about questions, reflect on experiences

Here are a few of the responsibilities that you'll have or need to delegate to others:

1. **Organize/schedule the meeting place(s).** You may be meeting at a church, at someone's house, or on a park bench. Just make sure you let everyone know where and when to meet. Among other resources, we've provided some e-vite, flier, and slide templates for you to use to communicate with your group members and promote your group meetings. You can find these resources at www.getrealgetclose.com.

2. **Play the intro video.** As a leader for the *I'd Like You More if You Were More like Me* small group experience, you'll have two options to receive your video content to help you kick off each session. If you bought the small group kit, you received a card with a link to www.getrealgetclose.com and an access code you can use each session to reach the videos. In addition, you can purchase the DVD with all six sessions on video from your

favorite retailer or directly from David C Cook at www
.davidccook.com. There is one brief intro video for each
session. These videos are meant to gather your group
together and get people thinking about the session's
topic in a general way. Each session's video features John
Ortberg, the author of the book *I'd Like You More if You
Were More like Me: Getting Real about Getting Close*, on
which this small group study is based. You'll find material
from that book quoted throughout your guide. Though
it's not necessary to have the book to participate in the
study, we strongly recommend that you and your group
members acquire copies of the book so everyone can go
deeper with the material and get the most out of these
sessions.

3. **Lead the group in exercises.** No sweatbands or pull-
up bars required. We've provided some simple exercises
throughout the study. Some of these will happen within
the group time, and some will happen in each member's
individual time. In either case, encourage the participation
of your group as much as you can. There are icebreaker
activities as well as "easy" exercises and "slightly awkward"
exercises. The "slightly awkward" ones tend to have you
getting more in each other's space and pushing past some
boundaries. (Just be glad we edited out all the "acutely
humiliating" exercises.)

4. **Facilitate the conversation.** This does not mean "deliver
an hour-long lecture," "research the biblical, theological,
and historical background for each question," or "fire

questions at your group boot-camp style." Though some of that might be fun for you, it probably won't lead to a successful session. We've given you questions here to use as a guide. As you study with your group, you'll learn what works best for your time together. Trust your instincts, listen, and allow space for the discussion to flow. This study is all about making deeper connections with one another—so anything that gets you there is all right with us.

5. **Keep the sessions alive.** Reach out to your members between meetings. Encourage them to use their guides in their personal study time and to think about some of the group discussions. This will help enrich the conversation and involvement the next time you gather together.

CROWD CONTROL TIPS

As the leader of your merry band of small group members, your job is to help the group travel through each session together. Think of yourself as the cruise host—you know the destination and you're trying to help passengers get there in the most enjoyable and satisfying way that you can. You can't do everything—it's highly likely that everyone is not going to be happy all the time. However, here are some examples of things you can do to help these sessions go well (and keep people from jumping ship).

Create a safe space. Right from the first few minutes of the first meeting, make it clear that what happens within the group should stay within the group, unless someone has given permission to do otherwise. Especially when talking about relationships and intimacy, people need to know that they aren't going to find their words plastered on a Facebook wall. You can even have everyone sign a covenant outlining the guiding principles of your group, if you so desire. Do what you can to make sure there is a level of trust and security established from the beginning.

Identify fears and apprehensions. You can discuss these at the beginning, but also keep an eye out as your sessions continue to see if any new fears are creeping in. Set aside a limited amount of time (no more than about five minutes) to let members talk about some reasons they might be reluctant to be involved in the group. Some people will want to vent about other experiences they've had. Try to keep bringing the focus back to what the specific fears are, and let everyone have a voice. You can break into someone's venting story in a simple way, such as "Thanks, Dave—you just reminded me of some good points to keep in mind as we go forward. Does anyone else have some ideas about how this group could work well together?"

Invite everyone. No, don't invite your whole town to be part of your group. But do invite everyone to the conversation. If someone has a tendency to talk too much, try to sit next to that person. Then you can just reach out and lightly touch his or her shoulder or hand when you need to break in. It's a quiet, non-embarrassing way to interrupt. Use a nonthreatening technique to invite those who are less inclined to talk; ask them to help you or acknowledge something about them. "Carol, help me think through this—what have you seen that might be a reason people fear intimacy?" "Bill, I can tell something has crossed your mind—what are you thinking about this?" Try not to accidentally shame or spotlight people by saying things like, "Sheryl, you've been as quiet as a miming mouse, let's hear from you now—the floor's yours!"

Manage your time and expectations. Talk with your group about how the goal of your time together is not to answer every question, but to have meaningful conversations and learn from one another. If you have a large group, it may help to break into smaller groups to go through the questions together. Suggestions are also provided about which Bible study questions to focus on when time is short. Remind your group members that not all the session material will happen within your group meeting time. Each of them has the opportunity to continue thinking through the topics in the personal study parts of the guides.

Pray continually. Pray before you meet with your group members, asking for wisdom to guide the others and for sensitivity to be aware of times when stressful situations or feelings might be weighing on people. Lead your group in prayer at the opening and closing of each session (or ask someone else to do so). Then also keep notes on things people bring up within the group and pray about those questions or needs. Pray often!

You might want to say a special prayer to ask for God's help as you are . . .

USING THE I-WORD

There's no use in beating around the bush. We have a problem. And that problem is brought to us by the letter *I*.

Our problem is intimacy. And we're not even talking yet about the concept. We have a problem with the *word*.

Say a couple is intimate and everyone nods knowingly. Say you have an intimate relationship with a friend and some eyebrows will go up (especially if you are married). Say you were handling business of an intimate nature and people might think you were washing your underwear.

So let's start right here and right now. Write the word *intimacy* in nice, big, fat letters right at the top of the next page. Make the word bold. Write it in red Sharpie. Use all caps. Then underneath that word write down all the words, phrases, adjectives, verbs, nouns, metaphors, images, etc. that come to mind when you think of intimacy. Take your time. Fill the page as much as you can. And when you're all finished, come back to this page and read the next bit.

Next Bit

Are you blushing yet? No worries. Red is a very flattering color. Let's keep going. At the top of the next blank page write the word *relationship*. Make it big and bold too. Use a different color if you like. Then underneath that word write down all the words, phrases, adjectives, verbs, nouns, metaphors, images, phone numbers, etc. that come to mind when you think of relationship. When you're finished doing that, go on to the following page.

_____

_____

_____

_____

_____

_____

_____

_____

_____

_____

_____

_____

_____

_____

_____

_____

_____

_____

All finished? Good job. Now one more thing. Go back and look at both of your pages and circle any words or ideas that showed up on both your Intimacy page and your Relationship page.

Did you have any circles? If so, consider how those circled items represent a connection between intimacy and relationship. If you don't have any circles, think about that for a minute. Why does intimacy seem separate from the concept of relationship for you?

What the Bible Says

The word *intimate* doesn't show up in the Bible much, but we can learn something about its meaning from the times that it does.

One occurrence comes in Job 19:19 (NIV), when Job is pouring out his lament after being rebuked by his friends. Job says, "All my intimate friends detest me; those I love have turned against me." Other translations use such words as *familiar*, *inward*, *closest*, *best*, and *secret*.

Another time in the book of Job, we see God's relationship with Job described as intimate:

> How I long for the months gone by,
> for the days when God watched over me,
> when his lamp shone on my head
> and by his light I walked through darkness!
> Oh, for the days when I was in my prime,
> when God's *intimate* friendship blessed my house,
> when the Almighty was still with me
> and my children were around me,
> when my path was drenched with cream

and the rock poured out for me streams of olive oil.

(Job 29:2-6, emphasis added)

Though Job certainly does have a flair for the dramatic, we can see here that he thinks of his relationship with God as having been very close—he felt God was watching over him, shining a light for every step of his way. He describes this time when he felt God's closeness as being a very rich, even luxurious time, when he was comfortable on every level.

So for Job and his peers, being intimate with someone meant having the kind of closeness that gave comfort and guidance—and having that intimacy taken away resulted in significant pain.

Besides the word itself showing up, there are many occurrences in the Bible of such close relationships—either between human beings, or between God and humankind. In his book, *I'd Like You More if You Were More like Me* (hereafter referred to as *I'd Like You More*), John Ortberg refers to the intimate relationship God had with Adam and Eve. God wanted to spend time with his creation—and he searched for them in the garden, asking "Where are you?" (Genesis 3:9). But because Eve and Adam had disobeyed God, they were afraid to see him. As Ortberg remarks, "the bonds of intimacy were broken." But God allowed them to hide, because "God doesn't want compliance; God wants intimacy. And intimacy cannot be coerced. Intimacy respects distance, but is not content with it. Intimacy, like God, asks, 'Where are you?' He's been asking that question ever since."

Think of one time in your life when you either felt like hiding from God or you felt separated from God in some way. Write about that time. What were you feeling and thinking? What caused you to want to hide? What did you think God would do?

_____

_____

_____

_____

_____

_____

_____

_____

_____

_____

_____

_____

_____

_____

_____

_____

_____

_____

_____

_____

Have you ever felt like God was asking, "Where are you?" Write about that experience.

_____

_____

_____

_____

_____

_____

_____

_____

_____

_____

_____

_____

_____

_____

_____

_____

_____

_____

_____

_____

_____

Intimacy is the thing that allows us to get real with people and with God. It's the thing that allows us to get really close. Close enough to get hurt.

And so, there's the other reason we all might squirm a little when we hear this word. It's not just that we so often have it linked with sex. It's that we know it means getting close enough to touch someone (either physically or metaphorically). And if you're close enough to touch someone, you're also close enough to be touched—or prodded, poked, and maybe even punched in the mouth.

Take some time to consider the people in your life who are close enough to move you, touch you, motivate you, or yes, even hurt you. List some of those people here—you can even use code names for them if you are worried about who might see this.

Fractures

Fear can create cracks in our relationships that make it hard to build intimacy. Take a moment and write down all the fears you have about being intimate with others. Fill in the cracks on this page with as many bad things as you can imagine that could possibly happen if you enter into a close relationship with someone. If I get intimate, I might _____ .

Foundations

Building intimacy can create a solid foundation that allows our relationships to weather the kinds of storms that destroy other, more shallow connections. On each of the blocks of this page, write down a good thing that comes from developing close friendships.

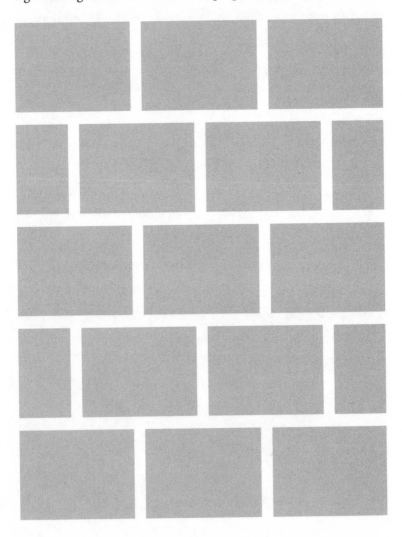

Consider these images of close relationships.

Cell phones not required: "The LORD would speak to Moses face to face, as one speaks to a friend" (Exodus 33:11).

More than a minute: "Jonathan said to David, 'Go in peace, for we have sworn friendship with each other in the name of the LORD, saying, "The LORD is witness between you and me, and between your descendants and my descendants forever"'" (1 Samuel 20:42).

Better than super glue: "One who has unreliable friends soon comes to ruin, but there is a friend who sticks closer than a brother" (Proverbs 18:24).

Ultimate intimacy, ultimate sacrifice: "Greater love has no one than this: to lay down one's life for one's friends" (John 15:13).

Portrait of a Friend

Think of a person you knew once or one you know now as a really close friend. Jot down some of the things that set the relationship apart from others. Did you have a secret handshake? Do you ask each other to check your teeth for spinach? Have you shared some sorrow or loss together? What makes that person a really close friend?

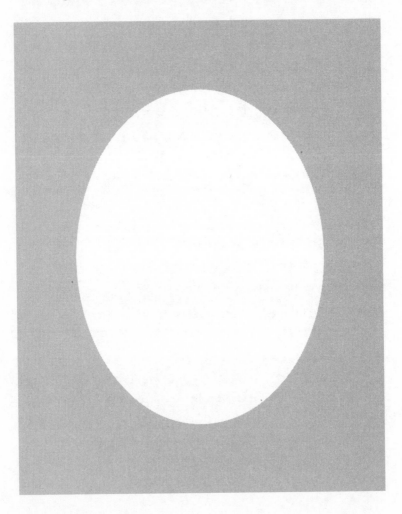

All those things that set your relationship with your close friend apart from any others are the things that create intimacy. As Ortberg put it, "the basic building blocks of intimacy—whether with God or other people—are shared experiences. For the most part, intimacy grows when one being invites another to share the many ordinary, and a few extraordinary, moments of their everyday life—and the invitation is returned."

Using the "I" Word with Others

So now that you've had some practice thinking about, processing, imagining, and saying out loud the word *intimacy* (and if you haven't said it out loud yet, go to the bathroom right now and look in the mirror and say "intimacy" ten times, slowly and clearly), you should be ready to not only use it with the members of your group, but to help them work through the following six sessions to understand how to make and maintain deeper connections with one another and with God.

How to Use the "I" Word Poorly

You probably *don't* want to put it on a big poster as the title of your study: "Intimate Study starts on Tuesday! Get ready to get close! Wear deodorant!"

Also, don't use it as the title of your Facebook group page: "First Christian Intimacy Club." That will just invite all sorts of questions and probably more than a few odd people.

Don't overuse the word—at least not at first. It's okay to make people a little uncomfortable, but ideally, you do want them to come back.

How to Use the "I" Word Well

Be real. Be honest about your own reservations and perspectives about intimacy.

Be the first to share a story. Nothing helps people to start talking about a tricky subject like a good story. Talk about a time you felt really close to someone or to God. Tell about a shared experience you had with someone: facing a fear, getting through a difficult problem, doing something that may or may not have been slightly illegal, or working on a project. Then ask if anyone else has had an experience like that. The stories will start to flow. And before you know it, you all will be sharing experiences together.

Share a meal. As Ortberg points out, "many of the moments that shape our lives end up being spent around a table." And just in case you need some dining ideas, we've got great group recipes, e-vites, Instagrammable images, and more available at www.getrealgetclose .com.

Use humor. Open up with an exercise similar to the one you just did. Divide your group into two groups. Tell one group to put the word *intimacy* at the top of its sheet of paper (or poster or whiteboard or whatever you have available) and then write down all the words, phrases, and images that come to mind. Tell the other group to do the same thing, using the word *relationship*. Just for fun, don't tell either group what the other one is doing. Then at the end of about three to five minutes, let groups take turns reading off the terms they have come up with. Laugh as you watch the "relationship" group come to the conclusion that the other group is rather overly-focused on sexuality. See—talking about intimacy can be fun!

Whatever you do, just be yourself, be open, listen, and learn. You are the leader, but no one said you had to be the BEST LEADER OF ALL TIME. You don't have to be perfect. In fact, it's probably better if you make some mistakes and let your group members see how you handle that.

So, are you ready? Feeling anxious? Excited?

Use the next couple of pages to jot down any worries you have, to-do lists, people to pray for, or anything else that's cluttering up your mind. As those great theologians En Vogue once said, "Free your mind, and the rest will follow."

_____

_____

_____

_____

_____

_____

_____

_____

_____

_____

_____

_____

AROUND THE TABLE

When I think about love, I think about a table.

IN GROUP

BE PREPARED TO
eat together

talk

draw

laugh

pray

MATERIALS
whiteboard, butcher paper, or poster board

dry-erase markers or colored pencils

scraps of paper

timer

OPEN UP

- Pray.
- Make introductions as needed.
- Make and/or enjoy a meal or snacks together. (Either you or the host of the group should provide instructions beforehand for what to bring.)
- Lead the group in an icebreaker activity (see below).
- Watch the optional video introduction.
- Discuss: What does the image of a family table represent to you?

Icebreaker Activity

Lead your group in the activity as described in the introduction. Divide members into two groups. Give each group a board and writing utensils. Let one group fill a board with words and concepts related to the word *relationship*, while the other group does the same for the word *intimacy*. Don't let the groups know what each of them is working on. At the end of three to five minutes, let each group take turns reading off the terms it has listed. Talk about which words or terms ended up on both boards and what that could mean.

CONNECT

John Ortberg reflects on how a table has been a symbol of love and relationships in his life: "For the people I grew up with, gathering around a table was the primary love language. If somebody got hurt, got sick, got married, bought a car, bought a house, had a crisis, had a baby, or died, that's what we'd do. There would always be the rich smell of coffee in the house (not Orange Mocha Frappuccino—just coffee), and we'd gather around the table to talk, laugh, and cry—*together*" (*I'd Like You More*).

So many activities in our lives—from the time we are children until we move out of our parents' houses and have tables of our own—take place around tables. We meet at tables to eat together, play cards, or make travel plans. Even in workplaces, people often meet around tables to listen to presentations, discuss ideas, and collaborate on projects. Jesus himself had some pretty interesting life experiences around tables—he even knocked a few over. Though not all these activities involve love, they all are ways of making connections.

Talk about it:

- What memorable experiences with people have you had that took place around a table?
- Who was involved?
- Where did you sit?
- What was it about the table that helped those connections happen?

Easy Group Exercise: Table Talk

If you have a large table or another flat surface, spread out some butcher paper to cover the surface (or use a large poster board). If necessary, break your group into smaller groups to perform this exercise. Distribute markers or colored pencils.

Let everyone have a chance to think about the questions provided below. Give group members time to draw images that come to mind when they think about their places at the table.

Think about it:

- What does your seat at your home table look like?
- Is your space at the table big or small? Do you have a lot of influence (take up a lot of space) or not very much?
- Are you quiet or loud around your table?
- Does your space look neat and tidy or loose and busy?
- Is your space at the table shared with others or do you have it all to yourself?

Listen as members of the group describe how they feel about their places at their tables.

Of course, the easiest way to keep your table tidy is not to let anyone sit there. But sometimes a table where messy people have spilled creates a memory that a tidy table never could.

Tables are places where many different people can come together and make connections. It's where relationships can start, grow, and even sometimes where they end. Life at the table can seem predictable and routine, or it can be surprising and unusual.

Whenever people sit and do life together, at some point or another interesting things are bound to happen. And that is just one of the many reasons why some people get uncomfortable at the idea of getting closer to others.

> *A table is a reminder that what really matters in life is relationships. We are hardwired for emotional connection to other people. We want to be known. We crave being loved. . . . We crave intimacy.*

As Ortberg points out, "Intimacy is a scary concept for a lot of people." And whether we call it intimacy or getting closer or making deeper connections, many people will still have some fears about knowing and being known by others.

Talk about it:

- What are some of those fears people have about getting close?
- What fears do you have?
- Where do these fears come from?

Slightly Awkward Group Exercise: Human Statues

Break up the group into pairs (or trios, if necessary). Each pair will be assigned to work with another pair. Pair 1 will be given a scene or activity to try to represent, which they must not reveal to Pair 2. Pair 1 will be the sculptors, and Pair 2 will be the statues. Without speaking, Pair 1 must arrange the persons in Pair 2 to look as if they are frozen in the scene or activity to which Pair 1 was assigned. Once everyone has created their statues, let the rest of the group guess what each pair represents. The "statues" can participate in the guessing, but must hold their positions until the guessing game is finished.

Here are some possible scenes or activities to use: catching a big fish, a nativity scene, posing on the red carpet for photographers, winning a rowing race, bowling a strike, hitting a hole in one, walking a dog, driving a chariot, Moses crossing the Red Sea, sacking a quarterback, Cinderella fitting into the glass slipper, fighting a Star Wars lightsaber battle, singing in church, Saul on the Damascus road, crossing the finish line of a marathon.

Part of the fun is having pairs come up with their statues as fast as possible, so write the scenes on paper ahead of time. Then have a timer ready and let one person from each Pair 1 group select a paper at the same time. Give the sculptors 60 seconds to create their statues. After the scenes have been guessed, play one more round in which the Pair 2 partners are the sculptors.

Think about it:
- Getting in each other's physical space can be uncomfortable and awkward.
- Getting in each other's emotional and spiritual space can be even messier!
- But getting in each other's lives and sharing experiences can be beautiful, funny, and life-changing.

While many of us fear intimacy with others, we wonder even more how in the world we are supposed to achieve intimacy with the almighty, universe-creator, death-defeater God. But God has been pursuing an intimate relationship with us from the very beginning. He is the one who designed us to need and want to be with others.

As we consider how we can create deeper connections with other people and with God, it will be helpful to look more closely at what intimacy is and what it isn't. Ortberg describes these points in detail in his book, but he sums them up pretty well in this statement: "Intimacy is not simply a feeling. It's not a mysterious experience that some people are born for and others are condemned to miss out on. It's not restricted to certain temperaments, or to married couples, or to 'feelers' on the Myers-Briggs continuum. And it's not something that mystically occurs the moment we say, 'I do.'"

Intimacy, Ortberg goes on to say, is sharing experiences—big ones, little ones, everyday ones. It's being present with others in those experiences and allowing time for that to happen. In other words, it's what Jesus did very well. So if we want to dig into what intimacy looks like, we can look at how Jesus interacted with his friends.

SOUND FAMILIAR?

John Ortberg told this story: "Not long ago at dinner, my body was at the same table with Nancy [my wife], but my attention was on the screen of my cell phone. A few minutes into the meal, I got a text—from Nancy—that read, 'I'm sitting right here.' Screens are useful, but they can forget their place. Screens are made for man; man is not made for screens."

BIBLE CONNECT

Work through some of these questions with your group, but don't feel pressured to talk about them all. Finish any questions you don't get to in your individual time later in the week. If you are short on time, focus on questions 1, 2, and 7–10.

1. Take a look at how Jesus made connections with his disciples. Read Mark 1:16-20 and 2:13-16. Where did Jesus find his first disciples? How would you describe the way he reached out to them? Jewish teachers and leaders normally trained and studied the Scriptures for years, and their students were trained under them. How might Jesus' approach to gathering disciples have seemed in contrast to the traditional way of Jewish teachers?

2. Read Mark 3:13-15. Why did Jesus appoint the Twelve?

3. As we read the Gospels, we can see that the disciples were with Jesus a lot. Go back and reread Mark 1:16-20 and 2:13-16. What were Jesus and his disciples doing together?

4. Find out more about how Jesus and his disciples spent time together. Read Mark 4:33-41. What did Jesus do for the disciples through what he said to them and what he demonstrated in front of them?

5. Part of being intimate with others means knowing them well enough to be able to challenge them. Read Mark 6:30-44. This passage starts out with the disciples coming to Jesus to tell him all that they had done. No doubt they wanted to impress Jesus with the amount of good they

had been doing. But Jesus wanted to stretch them some more. What monumental task did he ask them to do?

6. Once again, in Mark 6:45-52, Jesus challenges his friends. They did not understand what he was doing. In the storm on the lake, they didn't even recognize their friend. But Jesus did not give up on them. What did he do?

7. In Mark 8:27-38 we see Jesus having heart-to-heart talks with his disciples about his identity and theirs. What can we learn from those conversations? What does it mean to be close to Jesus? What does it take to follow him?

8. In Mark 10 we find Jesus confiding in his friends. He reveals a key element of developing intimacy with others and with God. Read verses 35-45. What is supposed to be different about those who know and are known by Jesus?

9. In Mark 14:1-42 we see four moving and slightly awkward portrayals of people demonstrating intimacy with Jesus: the woman with the perfume, Jesus at the Last Supper, Peter with Jesus, and Jesus and his disciples at Gethsemane. What was moving or emotional about these scenes? What was awkward?

10. Contrast the efforts of the woman with the perfume with those of the disciples in the garden. How do their actions demonstrate intimacy and closeness?

GO OUT

- Pray together.
- Discuss where and when the next meeting will be.
- Exchange contact information as needed.
- Use the space below to jot down a couple thoughts you want to remember and revisit before your next meeting.

_____

_____

_____

_____

_____

_____

_____

_____

_____

OUT OF GROUP

PRAY

As you go through this study, remember to stay in communication with God. Talk to him about your fears and questions. As specific people and relationships come to mind, bring your feelings about those people and experiences to Jesus. If you're ready, ask God to show you opportunities to get closer to specific people in your life.

Slightly Awkward Exercise 1

Ortberg points out how God has been pursuing us from the very beginning. He wants to have an intimate relationship with us. Consider the account in Genesis 3:1-10. When the man and woman ate the fruit, they realized they were naked and hid from God in their shame. God came walking in the garden, looking for Adam and Eve. He was searching for them. He wanted to be with them. So God called out, "Where are you?" (v. 9).

What is your "nakedness"—what are you afraid for God to see? What do you want to hide from God? Take a moment to write down what comes to mind on the figure shown on the next page.

Use your hand to cover the image and hide the words you've written. Now imagine God is walking down your street or down the hallway, just a short distance from where you are sitting right now. And he is calling out to you, "Where are you?" Can you take your hand away and show him what you've been hiding? Whether you are ready to show him or not, talk to him about what you're feeling. Take your time.

· · · · · · · · · ·

CONNECT AGAIN

Go back and think through the things you did and talked about with your group. Reflect on these things and write about your impressions.

What's something new you learned about the people in your group?

_____

_____

_____

_____

What's something you learned or revisited about yourself?

_____

_____

_____

_____

Pretend the shape on the next page represents the family table in your house when you were growing up. Take some crayons, colored pencils, markers, or other decorations and make this shape represent your feelings about that table from your childhood.

What is one thing you learned about intimacy or connecting with others during your time with your group?

_____

_____

_____

_____

What are some of your fears about getting closer to others?

_____

_____

_____

_____

Slightly Awkward Exercise 2

For many of us, connecting with others will not always come easily. Like most things that are good for us, it's something we have to practice—doing it over and over and over again until it becomes familiar and comfortable. Try practicing making a connection with someone this week. The next time you are waiting in line somewhere, pull out your phone and find a funny, touching, silly, or inspiring image to share with a stranger next to you: it could be a picture of your nephew with his birthday cake or a photo of your dog making a sad face or a silly meme you created. Invite the person next to you: "Since we're stuck here, do you want to see a funny picture of my hamster?" Later, reflect on what about that experience was uncomfortable for you. What felt good? Was it easy or hard for you to do? Why?

· · · · · · · · · · ·

As you look at news stories or scroll through Facebook this week, think about how relationships are represented in the media. What do you think intimacy looks like to most people? How is that the same as or different from your own idea of intimacy?

_____

_____

_____

_____

Read through the Bible verses that you talked about with your group. Be sure also to read through any that you didn't have time to discuss in the group. What does intimacy look like to Jesus? How is that the same as or different from your own idea of intimacy?

_____

_____

_____

_____

Ortberg points out several myths about intimacy in his book. One of those is that "Intimacy should be easy." Though you may have an easy time getting close to some people, that isn't going to be true for everyone, and maintaining any relationship takes time and work. What's the state of your relationships right now? Check your intimacy quotient with the following survey.

1. Do you have at least one person on whom you could call in times of personal distress?

   ___ Yes   ___ No

2. Do you have several people with whom you can visit with little advance warning—without apology?

   ___ Yes   ___ No

3. Do you have several people with whom you can share recreational activities?

   ___ Yes   ___ No

4. Do you have people who will lend you money or care for you in practical ways if the need arises?

   ___ Yes   ___ No

5. How likely are people to come to you when they need help?

   ___ Very likely ___ Somewhat likely ___ Not likely at all

6. Are people willing to be real around you?

   ___ Definitely ___ I think so ___ How would I know?

7. Are you able to have a crucial conversation with your friends about a difference of opinion without losing your sense of connectedness?

   ___ Absolutely ___ It depends ___ Not really

8. Are you comfortable living in disagreement (not anger)
   with someone?
   ___ Totally comfy
   ___ I'm mostly okay with it
   ___ No, I hate it!

9. What do you do when a relationship hits a bump in the
   road?
   ___ Work through it
   ___ Keep going without confronting it
   ___ Abandon the relationship

10. Who might find *you* to be a difficult person?

_____

11. Are you able to be real around others?
    ___ Yes ___ No ___ Don't know, haven't tried it

Look back over your answers. How would you describe your experience of intimacy right now in your life?

_____

_____

_____

*(Note: Ortberg offers more questions to go with each of the 11
Intimacy Myths he presents in his book.)*

Everything we've talked about in regards to getting closer to others also applies to our relationship to God. As Ortberg put it, "It's messy, sometimes seasonal, requires time and attention to flourish, is reciprocal by nature, fueled by love, and—here's the big one—it is possible for *everyone*."

This means that the same things that prevent us from building deeper connections with others can also get in the way of our relationship with God: too many distractions, not spending enough quality time together, not being fully present, not doing the work of getting to know him, and not communicating. Answer these questions to check out your current intimacy level with God:

1. How much are you experiencing intimacy with God these days?

   _____

   _____

2. What is your appetite for reading Scripture?

   _____

   _____

3. How naturally do you find yourself experiencing gratitude and expressing it to God?

   _____

   _____

4. Are you praying more or less than you used to?

   _____

   _____

5. Do you find worshipping God with others to be a stress-reliever or a stress-producer? Why?

6. Are you feeling more humble? more patient? more willing
    to give? If not, what do you think is holding you back in
    your growth in these areas?

    _____

    _____

7. When you are connected deeply with God, you care about
    the things God cares about. How often do you notice the
    needs of others and do something in response?

    _____

    _____

Slightly Awkward Exercise 3

Ortberg acknowledged that intimacy is big, "but it's built on small
moments." Do something this week that is small but meaningful for
someone with whom you have a relationship. Give a hug. Bring a
meal or a favorite snack to someone doing taxes, studying for a test,
or trying to get over a sickness. Surprise a person with a caffeinated
beverage on a miserable Monday morning. Or just pay a compliment! Take a photo to capture how you are creating your "small
moment" and share it with your group.

· · · · · · · · · ·

PRAY

Pray this prayer based on Philippians 1:9-11:

*God, please help my love for others to grow more and more in knowledge
of them and of you. Give me deep insights so that I can understand what*

is best to do for others and how I can keep my actions pure and blameless.
Let me harvest the fruit of Jesus so that all my relationships can bring
glory to you. Amen.

PREPARE

Do the following before your next group session:

- Read chapters 3, 4, and 5 of *I'd Like You More* (if you have a copy).
- Have a meal with one or several friends or family members at a table. Put away your screens and ask them to share some of their best memories of times around a table.
- Set up an email list, text group, or social media page for your group. Make sure all your group members are away of how to use the forum. Then be the first to post pics of those "small moments" you've experienced. Encourage your members to post their pics.
- See whether the host of the group has what they need for the next group meeting (if the host isn't you!).
- Think about this big question: Why do I crave connection?

LEADER PREP

Take some time to look through the next session and jot down your thoughts:

What top three points do I want to make sure to highlight?

_____

_____

_____

_____

_____

What things were brought up last time that might deserve more attention?

_____

_____

_____

_____

What special prayer needs does the group have at this time?

_____

_____

_____

_____

What Bible passages are jumping out at me?

_____

_____

_____

_____

_____

_____

What questions do I have about the meaning of these verses?

_____

_____

_____

_____

_____

Other thoughts?

_____

_____

_____

_____

_____

CREATED FOR CONNECTION

Vulnerability drives us to intimacy.

IN GROUP

BE PREPARED TO

eat together

talk

sketch

laugh

pray

MATERIALS

white paper plates, markers or pencils

blank sheets of paper

flat surfaces to draw on (such as large books)

small prizes (such as chocolate)

timer

OPEN UP

- Pray.
- Make and/or enjoy a meal or snacks together. (Either you or the host of the group should provide instructions beforehand for what to bring.)
- Lead the group in an icebreaker activity (see below).
- Watch the optional video introduction.
- Discuss: "The awareness of weakness leads us toward stronger community." Why do you agree or disagree with that statement?

Icebreaker Activity

Set the timer for three minutes. Instruct everyone that the objective of this activity is to form as large a group as possible. When you say "Go," participants are to form groups by finding people with which they share a minimum of two specific physical characteristics. They can get creative with their ideas, but they'll have to defend or demonstrate the characteristics at the end of the activity. Once participants have formed a group in which all members share the same two characteristics, they have to also then identify one way that each of them is different from all the others in that group. For example, a group may form of people who all have curly hair and can skip, but then each person will have to point out a physical characteristic about himself or herself that is not shared by anyone else in the group. Share the results at the end of the three minutes.

CONNECT

As John Ortberg notes, the need and significance of intimate connections in our lives becomes apparent from the moment we are born: "We hatch to attach" (*I'd Like You More*). For nine months, a baby shares the most intimate physical connection with his or her mother, and then they are separated. And after that separation—right from the start—the mother and father begin to try to understand the baby's requests for connection and to respond appropriately. It's a reflex—a baby cries, a parent soothes. And in that simple interaction, the foundation of identity, security, self-worth, connection, and attachment is laid.

When a baby seeks attention and gets a loving response, that baby takes in a lot of information. She learns that she is a separate person from the person staring back at her. She feels comforted and begins to associate comfort and safety with that person. She learns the difference between being in the presence of her comforter and being alone. She learns that her actions (crying, making noise) produce a consistent effect (someone appears, she gets held, etc.).

But none of this can occur until the baby is out of the womb—the bonding of parent and child can't really begin until there is the separation. It's a process that reflects the very beginnings of life—cells separating, multiplying, and bonding together. It's a process that reflects God's act of creation—separating dark and light, day and night, wet and dry, and so forth, so that he could join them all together to create a flourishing world. It's a process we recreate in a hundred different ways every week without even noticing we are doing it.

Talk about it:

- Talk about a time you've witnessed a baby being soothed (or soothing your own child). What about that interaction is valuable to you?
- What happens when a parent isn't able to soothe the baby right away?
- What is one of the first memories you have of knowing someone cared about you, or of feeling safe when an adult was around?

Easy Group Exercise: Detached Creation

Divide participants into two groups. Give each person a paper plate and a drawing untensil. Instruct everyone to hold the paper plates on top of their own heads and hold their drawing utensils with their drawing hands. Set the timer for 15 seconds. When you say "Go," everyone must draw on the paper plate the image of a baby, while holding the paper plate on his or her head the entire time. When time is up, let each group look at its drawings and select one drawing as the winner. You can then award a prize to the group with the best baby drawing.

Think about it:

- What made this exercise not-so-easy?
- Why is it so hard to create something you can't see?
- What did you rely on to help you finish the activity?
- What would have made it easier?

Parents don't always get the attachment thing down right away. Most parents misread their children's cues on a regular basis. Ortberg quoted one study that reported that mothers misunderstood the causes of their babies' distress about 70 percent of the time. But when people are committed to the relationship, they stick with it. They keep trying.

> *In our vulnerability, we run to them, and while we receive the joy of being comforted, they receive the joy of giving comfort.*

Of course, it's not all that surprising to realize that parents don't always understand the needs of their children. They still have trouble understanding one another as they grow up together. And we adults have trouble understanding other adults as well. We don't always communicate clearly. We miss hints. We forget. We ignore. We misinterpret. But in order for our attachment to one another to keep growing, we have to keep trying.

In Chapter 4 of *I'd Like You More*, Ortberg unpacks an idea that relational expert John Gottman calls "bids" for emotional connection: "It turns out that everyone—including you and me—is constantly sending out tiny little probes, emotional nanocrafts. . . . They travel at high speed, and it's easy to miss them. Those who are skillful at recognizing and responding to these probes have a great gift for cultivating intimate friendships. Those who are blind, or nonresponsive to them, often end up alone in the dark."

These tiny probes begin with our infant cries communicating fear, fatigue, hunger, discomfort, or loneliness. But as we develop, these simple cries become questions, comments, looks, touches, facial expressions—anything we send out that is asking someone to notice us, acknowledge us, value us, answer us—to recognize that we are separate persons wanting very much to connect with other persons. We are "I"s that want to be "we"s.

> *Each connection is like a deposit in an emotional bank account.*

Talk about it:

- Have you noticed these bids for intimacy happening in your life? What have you seen?
- Ortberg describes three main ways we can respond to someone's invitation to connect: 1) Accept. 2) Ignore. 3) Reject. What makes you more likely to accept someone's bid? (Consider something as simple as someone asking if you want to join them on a Starbucks run.) What makes you more likely to reject it?

Slightly Awkward Group Exercise: Blind Portraits

For this activity, divide your group into pairs and have them sit directly across from each other. Give each person a sheet of paper, a flat surface, and a drawing utensil. Don't worry—no artistic skill is required for this exercise. Set the timer for two minutes. Instruct pairs to place their sheets of paper in their laps or on a table. When you say "Go," everyone is to attempt to draw a portrait of his or her partner while keeping his or her eyes on the person's face and never looking at the paper. Participants should try to keep their pencils or markers on the pages at all times. When two minutes are finished, let everyone have some time to enjoy the portraits.

Think about it:
- What did you learn about your partner in this exercise?
- How did you learn those things?
- What, if anything, about performing this activity made you uncomfortable? Why?
- What did you learn about yourself through this exercise?

While we may receive thousands of tiny invitations to connect with others on a daily basis, there is someone else who is both receiving and sending billions of such invitations all the time—God. He's been looking to connect with us since he created us. Sometimes he may make grand invitations through magnificent sunsets on the ocean or the beauty of a misty mountain sunrise. Sometimes he whispers in a still, small voice and sometimes he thunders. Sometimes he gives us a house to build or a cup of water to offer or a hand to hold. Sometimes he just asks us to go for a walk in the garden.

Let's look at how God is inviting us to connect with him through his Word, and think about how we can respond.

SOUND FAMILIAR?

A couple is at a table sharing a meal. They're both looking at their screens, checking Facebook posts and e-mails from work.

"Look at this video of cats playing chess," she says.

He chuckles. Or doesn't. Or grunts. Or shakes his head. Or leans over to take a look.

Depending on how he responds to her bid, he either makes a tiny little intimacy deposit or he doesn't. (from *I'd Like You More*)

BIBLE CONNECT

Work through some of these questions with your group, but don't feel pressured to talk about them all. Finish any questions you don't get to in your individual time before the next session. If you are especially short on time, focus on questions 1, 3, 4, and 7.

1. Skim through chapters 1–3 of Genesis and write down some of the things that God separates and creates or joins together.

2. What good came out of these separations? Was there anything bad that came out of these separations?

3. The themes of separation and reunion appear throughout the story of God's relationship with his people. How do these themes connect to the message of the gospel?

4. "At its core, the gospel is the invitation to an intimate relationship with God" (*I'd Like You More*). How do you think most people respond to that invitation when they hear it? What do you think influences their responses?

5. In the last session, we looked at the way Jesus, the master of intimacy, interacted with his closest friends. Jesus also pursued intimate fellowship with many others, some of whom seemed to be intent on ignoring his invitations. In the Bible a lack of awareness, especially self-awareness, is often compared to blindness or living in the dark. We'll spend the next few questions looking at some who chose to be blind. First, let's consider poor Martha. Martha's complaint to Jesus regarding her sister is recorded for all time in Luke 10. And so is Jesus' response: "Martha, Martha, you are worried and upset about many things." In what ways was Martha blind to Jesus' invitation?

6. In Luke 12:13-15, a man asks Jesus to resolve a family dispute over an inheritance. But instead of giving financial advice, Jesus warns the man to be on guard against "all kinds of greed." Read these verses and the parable that follows. Talk about a) in what way the man was blind, and b) what Jesus invited him to do instead.

7. Read Luke 6:37-42. How can the kind of blindness represented in these verses be an obstacle to intimacy with others or with God? How could it block you from seeing bids for connection from others?

GO OUT
- Pray together.
- Discuss where and when the next meeting will be.
- Exchange contact information as needed.

- Use the space below to jot down thoughts you want to remember and revisit before your next meeting.

_____

_____

_____

_____

OUT OF GROUP

PRAY

As you go through this study, remember to stay in communication with God. Keep an eye out for specific invitations God may be offering you to connect with him, or opportunities he creates for you to connect with others. Ask God to focus your heart and mind to see these openings and invitations more clearly.

Slightly Awkward Exercise 1

When we are practicing a skill, it can be helpful to track our progress. Use the chart provided here to track bids for connection that you notice before the next group session. Remember that these bids can be subtle: a cashier asks if it is still raining outside, a coworker asks to borrow your phone charger, a friend laments the fact that he has to take his car in for repairs, a spouse asks you to pick up a gallon of milk on the way home. Record the bid, who made it, and how you responded.

BID FOR CONNECTION	WHO MADE IT	HOW I RESPONDED

CONNECT AGAIN

Go back and think through the things you did and talked about with your group. Reflect on these things and write about your impressions.

What's something new you learned about the people in your group?

_____

_____

_____

_____

What's something you learned or revisited about yourself?

_____

_____

_____

_____

Consider what you've learned about how we were designed for connection and about how that design shows up in the way we act, even from birth. Either from your own experience or from what you've seen in other families, list some of the positive effects that come from attachment. Then list some of the negative results that come from attachment disorder, which develops when parents do not respond appropriately to the needs of their children.

POSITIVE EFFECTS	NEGATIVE RESULTS

How does being aware of your need for intimacy affect your attitude about pursuing connections with others?

_____

_____

_____

_____

How do you think being more aware of yourself—of who you are, how you were designed, what you want, what you need, and how you feel—could help you pursue deeper connections with the people closest to you? How might this self-awareness also produce fears that could block you from pursuing connections with others? What can you do to get rid of those obstacles?

_____

_____

_____

_____

_____

_____

_____

Slightly Awkward Exercise 2

Use the provided chart to record the bids for connection that you send out to others. As you keep track of these bids, remember that sending and responding to bids for connection is something everyone is practicing all the time—the only man who mastered it was Jesus. If your bids are ignored or rejected, consider all the aspects of why that might have happened. Don't turn this into a bitterness chart!

BID FOR CONNECTION	WHO WAS IT FOR?	WHAT WAS THE RESPONSE?

Read through the Bible verses that you talked about with your group. Be sure also to read through any that you didn't have time to discuss. Think about how the gospel is an invitation to relationship with God. How have you responded to that invitation in the past? How are you responding to it today? What has affected your response?

_____

_____

_____

_____

_____

_____

_____

_____

Consider the kinds of blindness presented in the Bible and discussed by your group. Have you been afflicted by some kind of spiritual blindness? What is clouding your vision?

_____

_____

_____

_____

One of the tricky parts of pursuing deeper connections with others is the need to be aware of the person you are connecting with, and how he or she affects you and your relationships with others or with God. This is where practicing self-awareness becomes crucial. In Chapter 5 of _I'd Like You More_, Ortberg talks about the self that is elicited through our relationships with others. Each person in our lives either pulls us toward or away from our best selves. Think of some of the people in your life with whom you spend the most time. As you think of each one, ask yourself: How does my connection with this person have an impact on who I'm becoming?

_____

_____

_____

_____

_____

_____

_____

Of course, Jesus is not only the master of intimacy, but he's also the master of eliciting our best selves. What can you do this week to spend more time connecting with Jesus?

_____

_____

_____

_____

Slightly Awkward Exercise 3

We don't just send and receive bids for connection to and from other people every day; we also are always being offered opportunities to connect with our Father, God. Use this chart to record specific times when you recognized God was offering you an opportunity to connect with him, then record how you responded.

GOD'S BID FOR CONNECTION	WHEN?	HOW DID I RESPOND?

PRAY

As a metaphor for achieving self-awareness and getting rid of the obstacles that keep us from connecting with Jesus, John Ortberg refers to the story C. S. Lewis wrote of a boy named Eustace. Eustace was turned into a dragon, and Aslan the lion invited the boy to be remade. Ask Jesus to remove your dragon skin as you pray:

Jesus, thank you for providing a way for me to have an intimate relationship with you. Remove all my defensiveness, denial, and self-justification. Remove my pride and my fear. Open my eyes and make me see the truth about myself—and my sin. Even if it hurts me for a while, Lord, strip away any layers of falsehood I have built up to make myself look better in front of others. Help me to see myself as who you created me to be, as a child who wants to be attached to you. Purify my thoughts and help me identify my feelings. Give me the desire to belong to you wholly. Thank you for the free gift of grace that makes that possible. Amen.

PREPARE

Do the following before your next group session:

- Read chapters 6 and 7 of *I'd Like You More* (if you have a copy).
- Make sure to fill in your "bids for connection" charts.
- Consider using the hashtag #GodBid to post or tweet about times you noticed God inviting you to connect. Encourage your members to post too.
- See whether the host of the group has what they need for the next group meeting (if the host isn't you!).

- Think about this big question: Can the idea of misery loving company ever be a good thing?

LEADER PREP

Take some time to look through the next session and jot down your thoughts:

What top three points do I want to make sure to highlight?

_____

_____

_____

_____

_____

_____

What things were brought up last time that might deserve more attention?

_____

_____

_____

_____

_____

_____

What special prayer needs are going on in the group at this time?

_____

_____

_____

_____

_____

What Bible passages are jumping out at me?

_____

_____

_____

_____

_____

What questions do I have about the meaning of these verses?

_____

_____

_____

_____

_____

Other thoughts?

_____

_____

_____

_____

_____

COMPASSION AND COMMITMENT

It's not a bad thing to be an admirer of his. But he's looking for disciples.

IN GROUP

BE PREPARED TO
eat together

talk

remember

rejoice

mourn

pray

MATERIALS
computer and printer

paper and/or sheets of adhesive nametag labels (or self-adhesive notes, scissors, and tape)

timer

whiteboard (or poster board)
dry-erase markers
sheets of paper
pens or pencils

OPEN UP

- Pray.
- Make and/or enjoy a meal or snacks together. (Either you or the host of the group should provide instructions beforehand for what to bring.)
- Lead the group in an icebreaker activity (see below).
- Watch the optional video introduction.
- Discuss: Have you ever had a time when sharing with others in a (typically considered) negative activity turned into a positive, community-building moment? What happened?

Icebreaker Activity

Lead your group in a quick and fun pair-forming activity. The pairs created in this activity will do an exercise together later in the group time. For this activity, you'll have a little prep work to do. Before class, perform an online search for "emoji faces." If you are using Google, click on the Images tab and the search engine will bring up hundreds of images of emoji faces. You will need enough emoji faces to match the number of pairs created in your group. For example: if you have sixteen people, you'll need to select eight different emoji faces. If you have an odd number in your group, you will be the odd one out and simply join one of the pairs.

Once you have selected the faces you want—and you will want to choose ones that are fairly common—print out those images. Here's one way to print them:

1. Click on an image you want from the search window. A bigger version of it will appear.

2. On a PC, right-click on that image (for Macs, control-click). A window will come up that includes a "Copy Image" option. Click on that.

3. Then open a Microsoft Word blank document (or some other application similar to Word). Right-click anywhere in that document (or control-click) and choose Paste Special. You should see an option to paste it as an image file of some kind. Choose that; then your image should appear.

4. Click on a corner of the image to resize it. You'll want to make the image fairly small—about the size of a self-adhesive note. Once the image is the size you want, save your document.

5. Repeat the process of selecting an image from your search page, copying it, and pasting it into one document until you have all the different images you chose for your group to use. (If you're not all that tech-savvy, call on one of your group members sometime during the week to help you prep this part of your group time.)

All the images in your document should now be about the same size. Then print out two copies of your document. Cut out both sets of emoji faces. Tape the emoji faces onto adhesive nametag labels or self-adhesive notes (and yes, if you have super printing skills, you can of course print the emoji faces directly onto sheets of nametag labels—but the instructions for that get a little complicated, so you're on your own!).

When your group meets, hide the images until you are ready to lead members in this activity. Then invite them to stand up and face away from you. Warn them: NO peeking! Then stick the emoji face labels or notes onto their backs—high up on their backs where they won't be able to see them. One face per person, of course. Once everyone has been emojied (yes, we made that word up), instruct them this way: **Each of you has an emoji on your back. For every emoji, there is one matching emoji in the group. Your job is to discover your own emoji identity, and then find your matching partner. You may not speak. You may not draw pictures. You may approach another person, making a face that you think might match your emoji. The person will check your back. If you've made the correct face, the person will make that face also to indicate you got it right. If you got it wrong, the person will shake his or her head. Once you have discovered your correct emoji identity, you must then try to find your emoji partner as quickly as possible. You have one minute to discover your identity and find your partner. Go!**

CONNECT

In Chapter 6 of *I'd Like You More*, John Ortberg says, "The core secret to human connection is found in a single command given by the apostle Paul. If you follow this principle, you will never lack for intimate friendships. If you fail to follow it, you will never experience intimate relationships. . . . This principle is so simple that even a child can master it, and so challenging that even some geniuses never quite get it. What is the golden rule of intimacy? Here it is: 'Rejoice with those who rejoice; mourn with those who mourn'" (Romans 12:15).

Our ability to develop deep connections with others hangs on our ability to listen to, to watch for signs of, and to notice feelings—particularly the feelings of the other person (we're often pretty good at noticing our own). We can only share in someone's experience of joy or mourning if we are aware that they are having that experience. But awareness is not enough. We have to go one step further and not just act as a shoulder to cry on or wave a victory flag—we have to feel *with* the person. He cries, we cry (or in the case of the less teary among us, at least make a sad face and provide some tissues). She shouts for joy, we shout for joy (or again, for the quieter voices among us, we at least need to come up with a grin and a high five).

It may be helpful (especially later when we look at the book of Psalms) to think about this kind of active compassion as singing a song with a choir. Imagine the strange looks you'd get if you sang along with the upbeat, cheerful tune everyone else was singing (think "Jesus Loves Me"), but you chose a depressing minor key. Likewise, if everyone was singing a sorrowful requiem, you wouldn't dare slap on a cheesy grin and bounce about as if you were warbling "Happy Birthday"—at least, not unless you secretly wanted to get kicked out of your choir robe.

An act of compassion requires just that—acting as though *you* are the one who is suffering loss or being granted joy. It's an act of powerful imagination—using your own experiences to help you share in someone else's. And that makes it an act of intimacy.

Talk about it:

- Describe a time when you had a problem singing the same tune as others—either in rejoicing or mourning. What happened? Why was it difficult for you?

- Ortberg remarks that sharing joy increases joy and sharing pain decreases pain. What do you think about that? Would you agree or disagree?

- Consider a time when you were guilty of rejoicing when someone else was mourning. Why did that happen? (Keep in mind *mourning* here just means any sad experience: from dropping an ice cream cone to losing your whole ice cream truck business. Although those would be equally sad events, for sure.)

- Describe a time when you felt sad that someone else was experiencing joy. (Just think back to the most recent government elections of any significance in your region, and you'll probably be able to come up with some examples.) What would be good reasons for feeling that way?

Easy Group Exercise: Valley/Peak Moments

Use a whiteboard or a large poster board to record valley and peak moments that group members have experienced in the last week. Draw a large valley curve (a U) on the left side of the board. Make a mountain peak (a simple upside-down V will do) on the right side. Instruct the group this way: **Think about this past week. What were your valley moments—times when you felt disappointed or frustrated or angry or sad? What were your peak moments— when something went right, or you got an unexpected happy surprise, or you just felt great for no reason? Come up and write your valley or peak moments from last week on the board.** Once everyone has had time to write on the board, talk about some of the moments your group members offered. For the valley moments, ask them: Who was there for you at that time? For the peak moments, ask them: Who celebrated that with you?

Think about it:

- Who celebrates everyday victories and frustrations with you?
- If you don't share either of these things regularly, why not? What keeps you from telling someone about your experiences and how you feel about them?

- What role do trust and commitment play when you choose people with whom you can share experiences?

A good listener understands facts. An intimate listener understands feelings.

Sharing experiences of suffering or joy can make even strangers feel more bonded to each other. Joy tends to be contagious—which may be why we are commanded in the Bible to be joyful. Joy enhances the life of everyone in earshot. Have you ever witnessed someone who really enjoys her job? She spreads joy to everyone on staff—increasing the productivity and the morale of the whole company.

But what about mourning? What is the good in mourning together? The good there comes in the "together." Mourning with others means you take some of their burdens and carry them for a little while. "Mourning with" does not mean fixing problems, quoting scriptural hopefulness, or trying to get someone else to stop mourning. It means grieving, being sad. It means just sitting with a fellow human in his sorrow and letting him know he is not alone.

Tears are one of God's most brilliant intimacy inventions.

Talk about it:
- Have you ever had a hard time expressing your feelings in front of others? What happened?

- What makes it easier or harder for you to express your feelings to people with whom you have established, committed relationships?
- How can sharing in such experiences regularly create an atmosphere where commitment can happen?

Slightly Awkward Group Exercise:
Valley/Peak Life Graphs

Break up into partner pairs from the emoji-matching exercise. Make sure each person has a few sheets of paper and a pen. Instruct each person to draw a straight, horizontal line through the middle of a sheet of paper. That line represents the length of his or her life on earth so far. Have individuals make a point at the beginning of the line to represent birth. Everyone should then make other points along the line as they wish to represent life milestones: first day of school, graduation, college, start of career, marriage, births of offspring, deaths of significant people, etc. Pairs should then share with each other the big peak moments in their lives, from birth onward, along with the big valley moments in their lives. As they think about their valley and peak moments, individuals can draw lines to represent the ups and downs of their lives. See example on the next page. Have pairs talk about how those different moments in their lives affected their relationships with God and with other people.

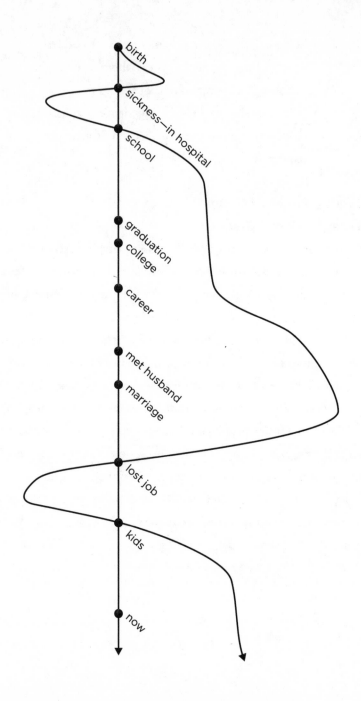

Think about it:

- The person you are and the life you lead are shaped by your valley and peak experiences.
- Your relationship with God can be affected by your valley and peak experiences.
- Sharing these experiences with others can help you find common ground where you think none exists.

Sharing in meaningful experiences with one another not only helps us relate to each other in the moment, but it also tests our trust of one another. *After I tell them about this, will they stay? Will they want to be with me even after the rejoicing is over?*

Commitment is the foundation of intimacy, because without commitment there can be no trust, and without trust, there can be no intimacy.

When we trust someone and commit to being that person's friend, spouse, business partner, parent, or 5K teammate, we create a space where we are free to share in more—and deeper—experiences. Those commitments also reflect our relationship with God. We are made in the image of a vowing, faithful, covenant-making God, who has created us for connection and who promises not to disconnect from us.

But commitment does come with certain costs. Ortberg refers to a description of these costs, as written by Lew Smedes: a loss of control, a loss of individuality, and a loss of freedom. However, Ortberg also notes that "commitment leads to a deeper freedom than all the other options and escape clauses in a commitment-phobic world" (*I'd Like You More*).

SOUND FAMILIAR?

Only human beings can make a promise. . . . Only human beings can say, "I will meet you next Tuesday. I will serve on that team with you. I will keep that secret. I will be your friend. I will pray for you. I will have your back. You can count on me." Dogs can't make that promise. If they could, they would—and they would die to keep it—but they can't. Cats can't make that promise. If they could, they would, and then they would break it, and they would laugh in your face in their quiet cat way. (from *I'd Like You More*)

BIBLE CONNECT

Work through some of these questions with your group, but don't feel pressured to talk about them all. Finish any questions you don't get to in your individual time before the next session. If you are short on time, focus on questions 1, 2, 5, and 7.

1.   If we want to have some practice rejoicing and mourning with others, we can find no better place than the book of Psalms. Read Psalm 23, where both joy and sorrow are represented. This psalm is often associated with mournful events such as the passing of loved ones—it is often read at funerals. But take a closer look. Write down all the imagery in this psalm that represents contentment or joy or gratitude. Now write down all the imagery that reflects

sorrow or mournful times. How would you describe the main focus of this psalm?

2. The shortest verse in the Bible is also one of the most powerful: "Jesus wept" (John 11:35). Read verses 11-37 and discuss why Jesus was so moved at this time. What does that tell us about Jesus? What does that tell us about mourning with others?

3. Read Psalm 95:1-7. What images does the psalmist use to express joy in his writing? Is he expecting to rejoice on his own?

4. Think about the kind of commitments God has made to his people. Read Genesis 15. What promises does God make to Abram in these verses? What did God do to show that he would keep his promises?

5. Now look at the kinds of commitments we should make to God. Read the story of Elijah and Elisha from 1 Kings 19:19-21. Elijah at this point is an old, tired, penniless prophet. From the text we see that Elisha is healthy and wealthy—he had twelve yoke of oxen! How does Elisha respond to Elijah when Elijah offers him his cloak (symbolizing his offer of the job of prophet to Elisha)? What does Elisha give up to go with Elijah? What does this show about Elisha's commitment to Elijah and to God? How would you describe his commitment?

6. Read about Jonathan and David's friendship in 1 Samuel 18:1-4; 19:1-7; 20. What did Jonathan risk for David? What did David risk? What promises did they make to each other?

7. Read Luke 9:23-25. What kind of commitment is Jesus talking about in these verses? How would you describe that commitment?

GO OUT

- Pray together.
- Discuss where and when the next meeting will be.
- Exchange contact information as needed.
- Use the space below to jot down what you want to remember and revisit before your next meeting.

_____

_____

_____

_____

OUT OF GROUP

PRAY

As you go through this study, remember to stay in communication with God. Thank God for the promises he has made to you. Thank him for the people in your life who rejoice and mourn with you. Ask him to show you the parts of your life where you are living as if you are not committed to him.

Slightly Awkward Exercise 1

Like other actions in this study, rejoicing and mourning with others won't necessarily come naturally to you. Practice rejoicing and mourning with others—even people you may not immediately feel happy or sorry for. When you are standing in line at the grocery or a convenience store, check out the headlines on the tabloid news or on magazine covers. Instead of feeling contempt or dismay toward the people featured, consider what it must be like to be involved in their lives. Put yourself in the shoes of the celebrities who are going through divorces, dealing with public revelations about their health issues, or having other intimate details of their lives put on display. Mourn with them in the stresses and pressures they are enduring. Rejoice over good news of good box office sales or awards.

CONNECT AGAIN

Go back and think through the things you did and talked about with your group. Reflect on these things and write about your impressions.

As you talked about each other's valley and peak moments, what's something new you learned about the people in your group?

_____

_____

_____

_____

What's something you learned or revisited about yourself? What did you learn from charting your peaks and valleys throughout your life?

_____

_____

_____

_____

During your time with your group in the last session, what is one thing you learned about intimacy or connecting with others? What increases intimacy? On what is intimacy built?

_____

_____

_____

_____

_____

Name one thing that keeps you from rejoicing or mourning with others. What can you do to get rid of this obstacle?

_____

_____

_____

_____

Fill out the provided chart to represent what you've experienced this week. On the first row, draw or write something to represent your main feeling about that day (happy, sad, angry, frustrated, confused, etc.). Then fill in the other rows with some details to say why that day was a peak or valley kind of day.

	SUN	MON	TUE	WED	THU	FRI	SAT
Your feelings							
^ or v ? Peak or valley?							
Who shared your experience with you?							

Slightly Awkward Exercise 2

Every day for the next five days, do this: As soon as you wake up, write down five simple things for which you are grateful. Record your lists here.

DAY 1	DAY 2	DAY 3	DAY 4	DAY 5
1.	1.	1.	1.	1.
2.	2.	2.	2.	2.
3.	3.	3.	3.	3.
4.	4.	4.	4.	4.
5.	5.	5.	5.	5.

Read through the Bible verses that you talked about with your group. Be sure also to read through any that you didn't have time to discuss in the group. If you have time, read more of the psalms. Jot down any interesting words or phrases that represent rejoicing or mourning.

_____

_____

_____

_____

Consider either something that you were happy about lately (new job, favorite team won the big game, son got all As, etc.) or something that you were sad or frustrated about (lost your favorite pen, didn't get the promotion you wanted, family goldfish died). Write your own psalm of celebration or of lamentation, expressing your feelings about this event. Jot down some ideas on these lines. Post your psalm somewhere where your group can see it.

_____

_____

_____

_____

_____

_____

Read Luke 9:23-25. What do you think these verses mean? What kind of commitment are you willing to make to Jesus right now?

_____

_____

_____

_____

_____

Slightly Awkward Exercise 3

Assess your commitment levels for different roles that you currently hold. Which roles do you find yourself asking these questions about?

1. How little can I do and still be called a _____?
   (Fill in the blank with a role you hold: good coach, good husband, good teacher, good supervisor, good mom, etc.)
2. How much longer do I have to do this?
3. Do I have to do this?

Which roles do you find yourself making these statements about?

1. I wonder how I can be a better _____.
   (Fill in the blank with a role you hold.)
2. I hope I get to do this forever.
3. It's my honor to do this.

If you have any roles that fall into the top category, what do you think you need to do to either change those roles or to change your attitude about them?

· · · · · · · · · ·

PRAY

John Ortberg tells how he once heard Dallas Willard give this advice in answer to someone who wanted to know how to grow spiritually: "Do the next right thing." Pray this prayer, asking God to help you do the next right thing.

God, please help me to see the next thing you have for me to do. And when I see it, help me to do it—even if it is difficult, or awkward, or annoying. Help me to work harder on the projects that I dislike. Help me to encourage people even when I don't feel encouraged. Help me to notice others and speak to them even when I don't feel like talking. Help me to use kind words when I'm frustrated. Help me to be patient with everyone. Help me to apologize first. I know I can't do these things on my own, Lord. Please help me. Amen.

PREPARE

Do the following before your next group session:
- Read chapters 8 and 9 of *I'd Like You More* (if you have a copy).
- Consider any commitments or promises that you have broken. What (if anything) can you do to make amends?
- Check your email/text/social media site to see if anyone has posted the psalms they wrote. Encourage group members to post their psalms so everyone can see them.
- See whether the host of the group has what they need for the next group meeting (if the host isn't you!).
- Think about this big question: What walls have I built between myself and others?

LEADER PREP

Take some time to look through the next session and jot down your thoughts:

What top three points do I want to make sure to highlight?

_____

_____

_____

_____

_____

What things were brought up last time that might deserve more attention?

_____

_____

_____

_____

_____

What special prayer needs does the group have at this time?

_____

_____

_____

_____

_____

What Bible passages are jumping out at me?

_____

_____

_____

_____

_____

_____

What questions do I have about the meaning of these verses?

_____

_____

_____

_____

_____

_____

Other thoughts?

_____

_____

_____

_____

_____

_____

WALLS AND CRACKS

Intimacy goes up when walls come down.

IN GROUP

BE PREPARED TO
eat together

talk

build

laugh

pray

MATERIALS
whiteboard (or poster board)

dry-erase markers

a few rolls of masking tape

2-3 old sheets

50-100 foam or plastic cups

spools of string

scrap paper (or old newspapers, phone books)

markers

(optional: prizes for winning team)

OPEN UP

- Pray.
- Make and/or enjoy a meal or snacks together. (Either you or the host of the group should provide instructions beforehand for what to bring.)
- Lead the group in an icebreaker activity (see below).
- Watch the optional video introduction.
- Discuss: How does the idea of fully revealing all your faults, sins, and weaknesses to someone make you feel? Does it appeal to you or does it make you want to run away? Why?

Icebreaker Activity

Start out with this really simple word-association-style activity. You'll need a board to write on and a marker. Draw a very simple brick wall on the board. Then ask the group to fill in the blank in this sentence: **My wall is _____.** You can either let your group shout out answers at will or take turns answering one-by-one. Write their answers in the bricks on the wall, one answer per brick. Lead into the lesson by saying that you'll talk more about the kinds and descriptions of these walls as you work through the lesson together.

CONNECT

"Our world is a world of walls," Ortberg notes in Chapter 8 of *I'd Like You More*. He talks about tangible walls and invisible walls of the heart. The walls of the heart are much harder to scale. Perhaps that is because the walls we put up around ourselves are specifically built to keep others out. As Ortberg puts it: "My ego blinds me to walls. My ego whispers to me that I am entitled to my life of privilege. It blinds me to the humanity of the kids across the counter at McDonald's, the person who takes my money at the gas station, the Vietnamese woman at Supercuts who cuts my hair."

When we build walls between ourselves and others we blind ourselves to our similarities and make it difficult, if not impossible, to make any kind of connections.

In *I'd Like You More*, Ortberg describes in detail different kinds of walls and the problems they produce—there are many stories and examples to explore. But in general, the problems all boil down to these four issues:

- Walls make me more disconnected.
- Walls make me more isolated.
- Walls make me lose perspective.
- Walls make me too comfortable with walls.

Talk about it:

- Have you ever felt like you were placed outside someone's wall? What was that like?

- What kinds of walls have you erected around yourself, and why?
- Be honest. Do you like your walls? Explain.

Easy Group Exercise: Build a Wall

For this exercise, you'll need four building materials: a few rolls of masking tape, 50-100 large plastic or foam cups, spools of string, two or three old sheets. You will also need at least 50 sheets of scrap paper per group (old newspaper or old telephone books could also work) and several markers for each group. This exercise has two parts to it. The first part is constructing the wall. The second part is delivering the message. For the first part of the exercise, place the four kinds of building materials in separate spots in the middle of the room. Divide the group into two teams. Then instruct them: **There are four kinds of building materials in the center of the room. Each team must select one person to pick up their building materials. When I say go, that person will have ten seconds to select two types of materials and bring them back to the team. Each team may select ONLY TWO types of materials. Once the materials are gathered, each team will have three minutes to construct the best wall they can. Ready, set, GO!** After the walls have been constructed, give each team their scrap papers. Then tell the teams: **When I say "Go," each team must write a word or phrase on each piece of paper and then try to get that paper to the other team. The rules are: 1) Each team must stay completely behind their wall. 2) No team members may keep papers from coming into their areas. 3) You have 30 seconds to complete the exercise. Ready, set, GO!** At the end of the paper war, have each team count all the papers that made it to their side—only papers that made it past their walls can be counted. Announce that the team that *received* the most papers on their side, won! Teams will probably be slightly surprised to discover this outcome. Explain that some walls keep valuable experiences out, and some let valuable experiences in. Ask the group: **What was your objective when you constructed your wall? Why? How would your wall have looked different if you had known the goal?**

Think about it:

- Think back to your childhood. What were the first walls you can remember experiencing?
- Why do you think people build walls?
- What do you think about this statement: "When we are connected to life and to each other, we thrive. When we are disconnected, we die"?

After building a wall together, consider the difference between building a purposeful wall with people and building a wall by yourself.

It's not the achievements, but the intimate moments of our lives that we remember.

Walls tend to represent strength in our culture, yet so often they are built as a result of fear. "We have to keep them out." "We can't let them get us." "We've got to protect our borders."

But God is the one who breaks down our walls—sometimes literally, as in the case of Jericho, when Joshua and his men marched around and around the city and the walls came tumbling down through the power of the Almighty. But more often God breaks down those walls around our hearts so that we can become vulnerable to him. When we are weak, he is strong.

God created us in his image. So, he gave us authority over all the earth. But he also created us to be utterly dependent on him. Naked. As Ortberg points out, "Our lives begin and end in vulnerability." And when God became man his life began and ended the same way—laid in a manger as an infant with the blood of birth wiped away, then laid in the tomb as a man with the blood of death wiped away.

> *We see the ultimate combination of vulnerability and authority in Jesus. . . . And this enables him to offer us ultimate intimacy.*

Talk about it:

- What fears do you have about becoming vulnerable to others?
- Where do those fears come from?
- What fears do you have about becoming vulnerable to God?

Slightly Awkward Group Exercise: Kryptonite

Have group members stay in the two teams you created before. Give each team a sheet of poster board and markers. Team should take some time to discuss each member's strengths by asking: *What do you do well? What do you excel at in your work life? In what parts of your relationships do you feel good most often? What people, places, or things make you feel stronger?* Make sure groups take time to listen to each person's strengths. Have one person in each group write down (clearly) on one side of the poster board all the strengths named. Allow some time for discussion; then have each team give its poster board to the other team. Ask each team to look at the other group's board and answer these questions: *If all the strengths on this board belonged to one superhero, what would that superhero's "kryptonite" be? What would be the ingredients of the object or qualities of a character that could weaken that superhero or destroy these strengths?* Encourage the groups to think creatively and draw a creature or object that would be that kryptonite. Make sure everyone gets a chance to contribute in some way to the creation. Write the particular powers of that kryptonite on the poster board. Then allow time for each group to present its kryptonite to the other group. Ask each team to evaluate and respond about how much damage the created kryptonite could do to its strengths.

Think about it:

- We often make the assumption that if we reveal our weaknesses to someone, that person might use the information against us. But God wants to use our weaknesses to make us stronger.
- Think about when your childhood fears started. What was happening at that time? What things contributed to these fears?

- How hard is it for you to believe that God can bring strength out of your weaknesses? Why?

Through breaking down our walls (or letting God tear them down) and embracing our vulnerability, we can become more like Christ. And in becoming more like Christ, we can get closer to achieving real, true intimacy with God and with each other.

SOUND FAMILIAR?

In a series of studies published in *Science*, researchers gave subjects a choice: sit alone with your thoughts for six to fifteen minutes or give yourself an electric shock. *One-fourth* of the women—and *two-thirds* of the men—chose the shock. One man shocked himself *190 times* in fifteen minutes. Some people would rather punish themselves with electric pain than be still. (from *I'd Like You More*)

BIBLE CONNECT

Work through some of these questions with your group, but don't feel pressured to talk about them all. Finish any questions you don't get to in your individual time later in the week. If you are short on time, focus on questions 5-8.

1. When we consider whether or not we should keep our walls, it may be good to look at Ephesians 2:11-22. What kind of wall is mentioned? Whom or what does the wall divide? What words would you pick out to illustrate God's desire concerning that wall?

2. Instead of being divided by a wall, what are the two groups in Ephesians 2 being joined and built together to become?

3. What does verse 18 assure us that we have?

4. We've learned that we are created for connection. In trying busily to feed that need for connection, we can get sucked into technology (phones, Internet, social media) to the extent that we actually build more walls—isolating ourselves from real people, face-to-face conversations, and physical touch. Technology can never satisfy our need for connection. Look at Psalm 139 to see how God satisfies that need instead. Write down what we can know about our Lord from what we read in verses 1, 2, 4, and 7-10.

5. The story of Jacob features both the struggle to find balance between authority and vulnerability and the kinds of walls that get built when pride and greed and insecurity dominate a relationship. Read about the beginning of Jacob's life in Genesis 25:21-28. What can you know about Jacob from this glimpse of his life? What kind of wall do you see being built between Jacob and his brother even early in their lives?

6. Read Genesis 27. What further building is done on the walls between Jacob and Esau in this chapter? Write down any words or phrases that create a picture of the kind of relationship that existed between the brothers, or between either of the sons and their parents.

7. Read Genesis 29:15-35. In what ways does the story of Rachel and Leah reflect some of the themes in the story

of Jacob and Esau? What fears shaped the actions Leah took?

8. Though the story of Jacob is filled with betrayal, dishonesty, hurt, and struggle, his story comes full circle in Genesis 32 and 33, when Jacob returns and must meet his brother Esau—the twin brother he has not seen since he betrayed Esau and ran away. Jacob is anxious (naturally) about meeting Esau. Read Genesis 33:1-11 to see what happened when they met. How did Esau greet his brother? Who was vulnerable in this scene? Who held authority?

GO OUT

- Pray together.
- Discuss where and when the next meeting will be.
- Exchange contact information as needed.
- Use the space below to jot down a couple thoughts you want to remember and revisit before your next meeting.

OUT OF GROUP

PRAY

As you go through this study, remember to stay in communication with God. Go to him with your questions about vulnerability, authority, and intimacy. Talk to him about walls you've built up between you and others. If you're ready, ask God to show you opportunities to get closer to specific people and how to tear down the walls that are getting in the way of reconciliation. Talk to him about healthy boundaries as well, and how to know the difference between a wall that is truly protecting you and one that is just blocking beneficial relationships.

Slightly Awkward Exercise 1

As you start your personal study time, read the first line of Psalm 46:10. Meditate on this statement by reading it over and over, removing a word or two each time as shown below. As you read the line each time, imagine that God is commanding you to be still. Think about what it means to be still in your busy life. It might mean: *Be still and don't answer that text.* Or it might mean: *Be still, the dishes will wait.* Or it might mean: *Be still; don't worry about the news headlines.* Or it might mean: *Be still; let me heal your anxious heart today.* Think about what it means to know that God is the one true God. As you leave the stillness of this place, consider how you might carry the stillness with you through the day—maybe by stilling angry thoughts in traffic or by stilling your tongue and not gossiping. Or maybe you take the stillness and knock something off your schedule today and spend more time with family instead. Consider how you can use stillness and the knowledge of who God is to improve one part of your day.

> Be still and know that I am God.
> Be still and know that I am.
> Be still and know.
> Be still.
> Be.

· · · · · · · · · ·

CONNECT AGAIN

Go back and think through the things you did and talked about with your group. Reflect on these things and write about your impressions.

What's something new you learned about the people in your group?

_____

_____

_____

_____

What's something you learned or revisited about yourself?

_____

_____

_____

_____

Consider the different kinds of walls you may have around you. Draw or write about those walls below. Give a brief history of how they came to be. Explain what you think your walls are blocking out.

_____

_____

_____

_____

What is something new you learned about connecting with others? What do you think about the idea of vulnerability being necessary for intimacy?

_____

_____

_____

_____

Slightly Awkward Exercise 2

Take this technology-use assessment and give it to someone else as well. So many of us use technology, either intentionally or unwittingly, as a wall to block interactions with actual people, face-to-face. Evaluate your technology usage and see where you might need to make some changes.

1. Do you sleep with your cell phone on your nightstand or in your bed?

2. Do your friends or does your spouse complain about you attending to a screen too much?

3. Do you check your phone first thing in the morning and last thing at night?

4. Do you feel bummed when you forget to bring your cell phone into the bathroom?

5. Do you feel anxious if you don't have Internet access for any period of time?

6. Have you practiced the art of secretly texting while maintaining eye contact?

7. Do you check your cell phone during business meetings, intimate dinners, or sermons?

8. Has anyone ever called you a phone/tech/screen addict?

If you answered yes to a majority (or all) of these, you may have a tech addiction problem. The good news is, you're not alone. But the bad news is, you're not alone. The thing about developing intimacy in your relationships means that you actually need to be present with one another—not just warm bodies in the same room. It means eye contact. It means focused attention for more than thirty seconds. So practice detaching from the phone this week and instead attaching to a person. Each time you are going to be someplace where you will need to interact with people—entering your office building, having dinner, talking to the drive-thru attendant—put your phone facedown on a surface and remove your hands from it, or put it into a pocket or purse. Put the phone away. Look people in the eye and smile or nod. Listen. Then after the interactions are finished, you may touch your phone again.

If you don't think you really look at your phone that much, get some of those small star stickers or yard sale price dot stickers. Every time you reach for your phone or look at your phone (other than when you are making or answering an actual necessary phone call or text), put a sticker on the back of it. If, by the end of the day, your phone is covered with stickers, you may need to make some changes.

· · · · · · · · · ·

What other habits or routines do you have that might be blocking interactions with people? Think about what your average day looks like. What's one small change you could make that might allow you to have more time to notice and act on someone's bid for connection with you?

_____

_____

_____

_____

Read through the Bible verses that you talked about with your group. Be sure also to read through any of the questions that you didn't have time to discuss. What did you learn about God's perspective on walls?

_____

_____

_____

_____

Read Ephesians 2:18. What does it mean to you to have access to God? Is that something you welcome or do you feel a little afraid to approach God? Explain the reasons for your feelings.

_____

_____

_____

_____

Read Matthew 25:34-40. What do you think about this statement: "Jesus is most present in the most vulnerable"?

_____

_____

_____

_____

Slightly Awkward Exercise 3

In the stories of Jacob and Esau and Rachel and Leah, we see that Jacob's interactions with his brother and father meant that he felt identified as Not-Esau. In a similar way, Leah must have felt identified as Not-Rachel. Feeling that you are defined in comparison to someone else—and that you fall short—puts a strain on relationships. But identifying that feeling is the first step toward healing.

Think about your relationships with family, friends, or coworkers. Do you feel like you are identified as Not-Someone? With what word or name would you replace "someone"?

Mentally remove from yourself the Not-Someone name tag. Instead, envision a tag that says, "I am _____." Fill in the blank with positive qualities that you display or beneficial roles that you play.

· · · · · · · · · ·

PRAY

Pray this prayer based on verses from Psalm 139:

Lord, search me and know me. Know all my ways. Hear my words before they reach my tongue. No matter where I go or how far I go, Lord, guide me with your hand. I praise you because I am fearfully and wonderfully made. Know my heart, Lord. Know what makes me anxious. Lead me in the way that is not wrapped up in things that don't matter, Lord. Lead me in your way that leads to everlasting life. Amen.

PREPARE

Do the following before your next session:

- Read chapters 10, 11, and 12 of *I'd Like You More* (if you have a copy).
- Remember to take the tech assessment, and practice putting your screen down to allow for more interactions with actual people. Text your group members reminders to do the assessment and practice screen-down time.
- See whether the host of the group has what they need for the next group meeting (if the host isn't you!).
- Think about this big question: Does sharing in suffering always lead to greater intimacy?

LEADER PREP

Take some time to look through the next session and jot down your thoughts:

What top three points do I want to make sure to highlight?

_____

_____

_____

_____

_____

What things were brought up last time that might deserve more attention?

_____

_____

_____

_____

_____

What special prayer needs are going on in the group at this time?

_____

_____

_____

_____

_____

What Bible passages are jumping out at me?

_____

_____

_____

_____

_____

_____

What questions do I have about the meaning of these verses?

_____

_____

_____

_____

_____

_____

Other thoughts?

_____

_____

_____

_____

_____

WOUNDS AND HEALING

We need an acceptance that's bigger than our rejections.

IN GROUP

BE PREPARED TO

eat together

talk

be in the dark

laugh

pray

MATERIALS

one chair

timer

gum ("glum") drops

two broken containers (see exercise instructions)

two rolls of duct tape

plastic tablecloth, water

OPEN UP

- Pray.
- Make and/or enjoy a meal or snacks together. (Either you or the host of the group should provide instructions beforehand for what to bring.)
- Lead the group in an icebreaker activity (see below).
- Watch the optional video introduction.
- Discuss: What impact does sharing together in suffering have on relationships? Explain.

Icebreaker Activity

Instruct group members to close their eyes. While their eyes are closed, ask them to think about these things: **Think about a recent struggle you experienced—mentally, physically, emotionally, or spiritually. Bring to your mind the feelings you had while you were going through it. What made it hard? Did you feel alone? Why? Now bring to your mind the faces of the people who helped you through that struggle. How did they help? How do you feel about the help they gave? If no one was there for you, why was that? Did you talk to God about your situation? Talk to him about it now.** Allow the group to keep their eyes closed for up to five minutes. Then instruct them to open their eyes and turn to the person or persons next to them and say the first word that comes to mind.

CONNECT

In this session we'll be talking about several big themes: suffering and hope, rejection and acceptance, rupture and repair. Though some of the wounds we will discuss happen at the hands of humans and some just happen, two things are true: they all sting and they all leave scars.

But what determines if suffering, rejection, or ruptures will lead to deeper connections with others or lead to isolation? What determines if our story ends in redemption or destruction? No matter the source of our pain, the outcome is largely up to us. How we come out of suffering and what we gain from it depends on our ability to meet God in the middle of it and hold on to others through it.

Talk about it:

- We have a tendency to want to create an inspirational story out of every tale of suffering. But sometimes suffering just causes damage. Talk about a time when something bad happened and there did not seem to be a silver lining.
- John Ortberg refers to *The Deep Down Dark*, the story of 33 Chilean miners who were trapped for 69 days. He then goes on to use that phrase as a metaphor for the place of suffering. In his description of what happened to the miners, he remarks, "They were at their best when life was at its worst." Can you think of a deep down dark experience you've had or have heard about where that was true—where people were at their best

when something terrible had happened? Describe
that experience. Why do you think people were
able to be at their best?

Easy Group Exercise: Cheer Up

Divide the group into two smaller groups. One group will be the
"sufferers." The other group will be the "encouragers." Place a chair
in the middle of a room. One by one, each of the sufferers must sit
in one of the chairs and face the group of encouragers. The sufferer
must put a sad or serious expression on his or her face. The goal of
the exercise is to try to get the sufferer to smile within 10 seconds.
The encouragers may do anything they want to achieve this goal,
but they cannot touch the sufferer. If the sufferer maintains the grim
expression for 10 seconds, he or she will become a semi-finalist. If
the sufferer breaks and smiles, he or she joins the encouragers. After
each of the sufferers has had a turn, start the next round, but this
time designate 30 seconds for each sufferer. If you still have sufferers
who have not been broken after the 30-second round, conduct one
more round, designating 60 seconds for each sufferer. If you still
have sufferers after that round, declare them Terminally Sad and give
them a bag of "glum" drops.

Think about it:

- This was just a silly game, but have you ever had
  the experience of someone trying to make you
  happy at a time when you were not feeling happy?
  How did the other person's efforts make you feel?

- What do you think: Is it better to try to make someone feel good or better to just listen to how they are feeling?

"Suffering changes people." This is something we hear often, and no doubt it is always true to some degree, depending on the severity of the suffering. But exactly how we change through suffering and how others deal with those changes determine how well our relationships survive. Ortberg discusses three ways that intimacy can build through suffering: by honoring differences, learning how best to respond to people who are suffering, and giving lots of patience.

If we want to see how to both deal with suffering and with sufferers well, we have an example in the Man of Sorrows. About him, Ortberg says: "On the cross, [Jesus] chose to *share* in the experiences that most isolate us—guilt, pain, hopelessness, and death. And the mysterious result is that we no longer have to be alone—or afraid—in those moments" (*I'd Like You More*).

Suffering with *is an act of tremendous intimacy.*

Some kinds of suffering we seem to bring on ourselves—through trying things and failing or not trying things for fear of failure. "We try out for teams we don't make; we apply for jobs we don't get; we pitch projects we can't sell. We don't wear clothes we love because we're afraid we'll look silly; we don't offer to use gifts God has given us because we're afraid we'll get turned down" (*I'd Like You More*).

When we experience rejection we may react in many different ways, from sorrow to anger to disappointment to eating ice cream. But probably the most damaging reaction to rejection we suffer is the feeling of shame. Shame takes root deep inside us and affects the way we look at ourselves. It is the condemning of self, by the self. It makes us feel that we will never be acceptable, that we will never be accepted.

Guilt causes us to feel bad about what we've done; *shame causes us to feel bad about* who we are.

Healing from that kind of suffering can come—we see it come in the story of the Samaritan woman. A woman who had been shaped by her life choices came to the well and drew up a bucket of transformation. Or as Ortberg puts it: "This is a woman who came to the well with a bucket and went home with the well." And that same living water that refreshed her soul and renewed her heart is the same living water we can drink from today. It's the same water that brings us this revelation: "Therefore, there is now no condemnation for those who are in Christ Jesus, because through Christ Jesus the law of the Spirit who gives life has set you free from the law of sin and death" (Romans 8:1, 2). No condemnation. Not from others. Not from yourself. Not from God.

Talk about it:

- Think back to when you were a small child. When was the first time you remember feeling ashamed?

- How did that shame go away? (Or did it?)
- Talk about a recent rejection that you suffered. Whether it was big or small in your eyes, why did it bother you? How did suffering that rejection affect your relationships?

Slightly Awkward Group Exercise: Shattered

Before class, obtain two large vases or other containers (ideally at least 12 inches tall or wide). The containers should be made of a material that can break or be torn, but not glass (for safety concerns). Find containers at a thrift store or use unwanted items. Prior to your meeting, break these containers into several pieces. You could put the containers in a garbage bag and smash them with a hammer or tear them apart or cut them apart (depending on what materials they are made of). It is okay to allow the pieces of the two containers to be mixed together, but try not to make the pieces too small.

During class, divide into two groups. Place a plastic tablecloth down on a table or floor. Bring out the container pieces and place them on the tablecloth. Give each group a roll of duct tape. Tell them that there are pieces to two containers in the pile. Each group must choose a container to work on, find as many pieces of it as possible, and try to put those pieces back together. Before a person can add a piece to the container, he or she should give the piece a name that represents a ruptured relationship with a friend, spouse, family member, or coworker. Group members can share the words for their pieces and tell as much as they wish about how the ruptures occurred, and how they were or could be mended. Once each group has put its container together again as best as it can, have groups fill the containers with water and see how well they hold together. Talk about what happens when ruptures are repaired. Do relationships get stronger or are there still weaknesses?

Think about it:

- Some ruptures in relationships are worse than others. What kinds of issues are hard for you to get over?
- Ortberg asks this question in *I'd Like You More*: "Is it really possible to have honest conflict and still remain connected?" How would you answer that question?

Every relationship experiences ruptures from time to time. What determines ongoing intimacy is what happens next.

In most cases the wounds we receive from suffering and rejection are the places from which relationship ruptures grow and bloom. Even when we heal from those wounds, the scars and the memories are still there—and the pain can get easily reactivated by a stressful argument, a harsh retort, or even the most minor slight.

Ruptures within relationships are going to happen—we need to be okay with that truth. But what really matters is what we do afterward. Do we move away from, move against, or move toward the other person?

When we sin we rupture our relationship with God. And God shows us what to do afterward. He moves toward us. He moved toward his people in the garden ("Where are you?"); he moved toward his people after the flood (that promise tied with a rainbow); and he moved toward us under a star, in a manger, across a sea, and on the cross.

SOUND FAMILIAR?

Harvard researcher Shawn Achor once talked to a tax auditor who was very depressed. As they were talking about why, the auditor mentioned that one day during a break at work, he made an Excel spreadsheet listing all the mistakes his wife had made during the past six weeks. (I am not making this up.) (from *I'd Like You More*)

BIBLE CONNECT

Work through some of these questions with your group, but don't feel pressured to talk about them all. Finish any questions you don't get to in your individual time later in the week. If you are short on time, focus on questions 1, 4, 6, 7, and 9.

1. The story of Joseph shows us a young man who learned about empathy through suffering. Read Genesis 37:1-11. How did Joseph's brothers feel about him? How did Joseph feel about his brothers?

2. Joseph was betrayed by his brothers, sold into slavery, betrayed by his master's wife, and put in prison. Read Genesis 39:20-23. Who was with Joseph in his suffering? What effect did that have on Joseph?

3. Read Genesis 40:6, 7. How do these verses show a change in Joseph from the boy who told his dreams to his brothers?

4. Read Genesis 43:29-34; 45:1-7, 14, 15; 50:15-21. What can you learn from these verses about what effects suffering, rejection, and ruptured relationships had on these men?

5. Ortberg discusses the difference between grumbling and groaning as expressions of suffering. In our relationships with each other, groaning means raising our complaints with the person who is at the heart of our conflict. Grumbling means talking about that person to anyone else. In our relationships with God, groaning means lifting our laments about our suffering directly to God. Grumbling would be complaining about our disappointment with God to anyone else who would listen. Where can you find groaning and grumbling in Joseph's story? Why does groaning build intimacy while grumbling erodes intimacy?

6. Many generations after the time of Joseph, a boy-meets-girl story unfolds in the town of Sychar, near the land Jacob had given to Joseph. It's the story of Jesus meeting a Samaritan woman in the heat of the day. Read John 4:1-30, 39-42 and answer the following question: Jesus made a "bid" to connect with the woman. What was his bid, and how did she respond?

7. Think about these characteristics of the Samaritan woman:
   - She was poor. A woman of means would have had a servant do the work of hauling water.
   - She was trying to avoid society. People would generally go fetch the water during the cooler parts of the day, yet here she was at noon.

- She had not only experienced societal rejection (from Jews and from her own town), she had experienced personal suffering through her broken relationships with men.

  Look carefully at what Jesus said and did in this story. What can we learn from the way he addressed her various levels of suffering and rejection? Consider what another rabbi might have done in his place (Samaritan women were considered unclean by the Jews). What might that interaction have looked like?

8. The Samaritan woman went from hiding and dodging in her shame to speaking out. Though we don't know what happened with her and her not-husband, what can we observe about how her relationships changed?

9. What do you see in the story of the Samaritan woman that reminds you of your own situation? What is different? How do you think you would have responded to Jesus' bid to connect?

GO OUT

- Pray together.
- Discuss where and when the next meeting will be.
- Exchange contact information as needed.
- Use the space below to jot down a couple thoughts you want to remember and revisit before your next meeting.

_____

_____

_____

_____

OUT OF GROUP

PRAY

As you go through this study, remember to stay in communication with God. If you are currently going through a period of suffering, ask God to sit with you in that suffering. Ask him to send someone to care for you through that suffering. If you are nursing the sting of rejection, talk to God about your feelings—groan to God about your disappointment, frustration, and shame. Honestly ask God to reveal to you ways that you have inflicted suffering on others or ways that you have rejected others. Ask forgiveness for times that you have grumbled about God or other people.

Slightly Awkward Exercise 1

Take on the role of a suffering detector. Pick a day when you know you will have to interact often with other people. As you go through your day remember to pay attention to every person you meet: the salesperson on the phone, your children, the dry cleaner clerk, the bus driver, the soccer coach, your spouse, etc. Listen to their responses to your question, "How are you doing today?" Don't just accept "Fine" as an answer and keep walking. Listen and ask a follow-up question such as "Really? You don't sound so fine—has something gone wrong today?" Or "Glad to hear it—what's been going well today?"

· · · · · · · · · ·

CONNECT AGAIN

Go back and think through the things you did and talked about with your group. Reflect on these things and write about your impressions.

What's something new you learned about the people in your group?

_____

_____

_____

_____

What's something you learned or revisited about yourself?

_____

_____

_____

_____

What have you learned in this session that will help you make deeper connections with people and increase intimacy? What have you learned about ways of eroding intimacy?

_____

_____

_____

_____

_____

_____

_____

Make a list of groans for your week. What things are causing you to feel bad? Circle the ones that you've grumbled to others about. What could you do instead of grumbling?

_____

_____

_____

_____

_____

_____

_____

Slightly Awkward Exercise 2

Practice some rejection therapy. In *I'd Like You More*, Ortberg tells the story of Jia Jiang, a man who had experienced various kinds of rejection. He didn't want his fear of rejection to keep him from taking risks, so he tried a behavioral treatment called "rejection therapy." The idea is that you make outrageous requests—ones you know will be rejected—so that you eventually get used to hearing the word no, and that word starts to lose its power. Two examples of what Jia Jiang asked for are a burger refill at a fast-food restaurant and a German Shepherd haircut at a PetSmart. What outrageous requests can you make? Try making ten outrageous requests this week. If you need help with ideas, ask some fellow group members. Take some selfies to document your exercises of rejection therapy and post those so your group can see them.

· · · · · · · · · ·

Write down all the sources of shame that you are currently carrying around with you. It could be shame about being abandoned by your father when you were a child. Or shame about losing a job. Or you could just feel ashamed of cheating on your diet. Or about bad feelings you keep having toward someone you work with. Over the top of every entry on your list write the words "no condemnation" (making the original entry virtually unreadable). Next to each entry on your list, write one positive thing you know about yourself.

_____

_____

_____

_____

_____

_____

_____

_____

_____

_____

_____

Read through the Bible verses that you talked about with your group. Be sure also to read through any that you didn't have time to discuss in the group. What struck you about the story of Joseph?

_____

_____

_____

What stood out for you about the story of the Samaritan woman?

_____

_____

_____

_____

Read Romans 15:7. What kind of acceptance do you have in Christ today? What kind of acceptance do you need to offer to someone else?

_____

_____

_____

_____

Slightly Awkward Exercise 3

Perform a gratitude audit on one of your close relationships. Make a copy of the chart on the next page, or fill it in using pencil so that you can erase and use it again, if you wish. Write your person's name on the line at the top. Then fill out the rest of the chart, thinking of different qualities or facts or experiences of that person that you are grateful for. Then take a picture of that chart and send it to the person the chart is about. Try doing this every week and see what happens!

THINGS I AM GRATEFUL FOR ABOUT _____	
Something true.	
Something noble.	
Something right.	
Something pure.	
Something lovely.	
Something admirable.	
Something excellent.	
Something praiseworthy.	

Before your next session—as you interact with friends, roommates, your spouse, your kid, your parent, your boss, or anyone else close to you—consider John Ortberg's strategies for moving from rupture in relationships to repair. Consider even small ruptures, since small ones build up into bigger ones over time.

1) Stop. When you feel your emotions rising, take a break. Go for a walk. Go to the bathroom. Calm down.

2) Ask. When you've calmed yourself, ask these two questions: Why am I angry/frustrated/sad/feeling what I'm feeling? and What do I want?

3) Caution. Consider your approach carefully. Remember that how you begin a conversation can significantly affect how it will end.

4) Yield. Slow down enough to recognize what the other person is experiencing right now.

Try reminding yourself of these symbols as you interact with people this week. Jot some notes down here so you can remember what worked and what didn't.

_____

_____

_____

_____

_____

_____

_____

PRAY

Pray this prayer:

Man of Sorrows, you understand my suffering more than I do. You experienced the pain of being rejected by the world. Help me to strip away any masks that I use to hide my pain or shame. Help me to let go of my insecurity. Help me to be honest with those who are closest to me about the cause of my negative feelings. Help me to stop condemning myself. Enable me to separate my regret about what I've done from my confidence about who you've created me to be. Help me to rest in that confidence as I seek to repair and grow my relationships with the people I care about the most. Amen.

PREPARE

Do the following before your next group session:

- Read chapters 13 and 14 of *I'd Like You More* (if you have a copy).
- Continue to practice being a suffering detector whenever you can and encourage your group members to do the same.
- Check your email/text/social media site to see if anyone has posted evidence of his or her rejection-therapy exercises. Encourage your group members to share their experiences with each other.
- See whether the host of the group has what they need for the next group meeting (if the host isn't you!).
- Think about this big question: Who will cry at my funeral?

LEADER PREP

Take some time to look through the next session and jot down your thoughts:

What top three points do I want to make sure to highlight?

_____

_____

_____

_____

What things were brought up last time that might deserve more attention?

_____

_____

_____

_____

What special prayer needs does the group have at this time?

_____

_____

_____

_____

_____

What Bible passages are jumping out at me?

_____

_____

_____

_____

_____

What questions do I have about the meaning of these verses?

_____

_____

_____

_____

_____

Other thoughts?

_____

_____

_____

_____

REAL AND CLOSE

When I think about love, I think about a table.
But it's not healthy for us to sit at the table forever.

IN GROUP

BE PREPARED TO

eat together

talk

get real

serve

laugh

pray

MATERIALS

paper

pencils

timer

service project supplies (as needed)

OPEN UP

- Pray.
- Make and/or enjoy a meal or snacks together. (Either you or the host of the group should provide instructions beforehand for what to bring.)
- Lead the group in an icebreaker activity (see below).
- Watch the optional video introduction.
- Discuss: Does sharing our best friends with others cause us to grow closer together or does it cause us to lose our best friends?

Icebreaker Activity

Explain that in times long ago and in certain cultures, it was common for wealthy people to pay for mourners to attend funerals. In fact, this practice still goes on today in some places. Ask the group: **If money were not an issue, who would you pay to mourn at your funeral?** Consider celebrities, sports stars, favorite actors, politicians, or just people you would really want to be there who might not come unless they were given money to do so. Have each person make a list of his or her top five mourners and share the list with the group.

CONNECT

This is our last session! But thankfully, it isn't the end of our journey to closer relationships and deeper connections. Instead, this is just the beginning.

We're sure you've already started using some of the ideas in this study to reach out, to connect, to commit, to tear down, and to repair. And by now you can probably say *intimacy* without hesitating even slightly or mumbling it under your breath.

We started out this journey at the table. It was good to spend time there—listening together, learning about one another, laughing, and sharing in some good food for thought (and for the stomach). But it's time to push our chairs back and move on.

But where will we go first? And who will go with us?

In Chapter 13 of *I'd Like You More*, Ortberg discusses the idea of thinking about who will cry at your funeral. This isn't some kind of morbid game, but it's a way to focus on what really matters. And who really matters. It helps us prioritize the time we spend with people and the energy we put into our relationships.

Talk about it:

- In our intro activity, we talked about who would be at our funeral. But who will not be there? Specifically, of the people we spend time thinking about, reading about, watching on TV, working with, bumping into, and so forth in any given year, which of those people are we really investing in? And which ones should we be investing less time and energy in? (For example, those people on Netflix I spent 8 hours of my life with last Saturday probably won't show up to my funeral.)
- Am I giving the best of my time and my life to the people who will miss me when I'm gone?

- How am I serving the people that I care about
  the most?

Easy Group Exercise: Speed Ritual Practice

Explain to the group that in *I'd Like You More*, John Ortberg describes five rituals that author Martin Seligman recommends that people in any kind of relationship observe on a daily or weekly basis. These rituals are: beginnings, reunions, affection, one weekly date, and appreciation. Today you will be performing just three of these rituals, but in an accelerated and abbreviated form. Think of it as the speed-dating version of relational rituals. Instruct everyone to find a partner (you as leader can be someone's partner if you have an odd number of group members). Then explain that when you say "Go," all group members must get up and try to perform a positive **beginning** (a greeting or opening question such as "How are you?"), deliver some expression of friendly **affection** (a high-five, hug, handshake, etc.), and express **appreciation** (a compliment about or thank-you for something) to their partners. (If some of your members are unable to move around easily, make sure they can stay comfortably seated while others come to them.) Each person must perform these three acts before they move to the next person of their choosing. Try to see how many people you can get to in the allotted time of five minutes.

Think about it:

- What is my typical greeting to the people who are
  closest to me?
- How have I been showing appreciation to people
  I care about?

- When I'm gone for a week, does anyone really
  notice? When other people are gone, do I notice?

When Jesus was having his Last Supper with his friends, there came a point when—as sometimes happens between brothers and friends at the table—a quarrel broke out: Who was the greatest? Jesus answered the dispute with "Who is greater, the one who is at the table or the one who serves? Is it not the one who is at the table? But I am among you as one who serves" (Luke 22:27). He then told them he was conferring on them a kingdom, with the implication being that in this kingdom, they—like him—would serve.

And then Jesus said, "Wanna go for a walk?" (or something like that), and they went out to the Mount of Olives—for centuries the source of the oil used to anoint kings and high priests. And there this King of kings and our intimate high priest knelt on the ground and prayed so earnestly, sweat poured from his brow like drops of blood. And his friends were there with him in his suffering. And he was there . . . with all of us in *our* suffering.

Perhaps he thought, *Who will cry at my funeral?* And, *Will they remember I said I was coming back?*

He loves the worst person in his world more than you love the best person in yours.

In some of his last words to his best friends, Jesus made himself clear. The way to get real—to get real about getting close, to get real about having deep, loving, eternity-shaped connections with people—is to serve one another.

Ortberg puts it this way: "The fellowship of the early church centered on the dinner table. They shared the Lord's supper there. It was a place of great intimacy. But the measure of the greatness of their community was not the experience of intimacy; it was the extent to which their intimacy with God and with one another overflowed to the blessing of those not yet at the table" (*I'd Like You More*).

> *It may not be your fault, but it certainly is your time.*

There's a world out there that is hurting and suffering—alone in the dark. It's a world that's waiting for us to get up from the table. Waiting for us to go and make disciples, to tell them that Jesus is with us—always, and to the very end.

Talk about it:

- Ortberg refers to the act of having a relationship with those outside your circle of intimacy as "outimacy." He says, "Remember, *intimacy* without *outimacy* leads to stagnation and death. Once you have experienced true intimacy, it is your great commission to share it with others." What do you think about that? How is it good for a community to move outside that community?

- Is the level of happiness within a community always a good measure of success? Why or why not? How true do you think this statement is: "People who are deeply connected are deeply happy"?

- How could the church do a better job at being the church in the world?

Slightly Awkward Group Exercise: It's Our Time

Before class, communicate with your group members to see what you could do together as a group to serve others. You may decide to create gift bags for homeless people (with resealable bags full of useful items such as deodorant, socks, toothpaste, coins for laundry machines, protein snacks, bottles of water, etc.), collect clothing items to donate to a local shelter, or serve at a soup kitchen. There are many ways your group can serve others. You may choose to serve together during your regular group time, or just use that time to collect supplies for the activity and then serve together at another time. Remember to do these two things as you go to serve: 1) Pray together as a group; 2) Talk about the experience afterward. How did it feel to serve in this way? What would you do again? What would you do differently? What did you learn?

Think about it:

- How do you feel when you are serving others?
- What are some habits or practices in your church family that might make it easy to get caught up in just talking with and serving one another inside the church—instead of going out?

- Think about this statement: "When it comes to love . . . it turns out giving is the only path to receiving."

We can find many examples in the Bible of people who shared experiences with each other, developed a bond, and then went out and served others. Of course, the greatest example of this is Jesus. "If intimacy is shared experience, then the Incarnation is its greatest expression, its highest articulation, its deepest sacrifice" (Ortberg, *I'd Like You More*). Jesus not only wrote the last word on intimacy, he was the Word. And in his fleshy, messy, broken, and scarred self, he showed us what it looks like to live a fully committed life—a life so real, it hurts. And he showed us how to get real too.

♡ SOUND FAMILIAR?

In *I'd Like You More*, John Ortberg envisions where we can see love in the world: "It's in the marriage and parenting. It's in the family and friends. It's in the murmur of my parents' voices when I'm a drowsy little boy in the back seat of the car and all is right with the world. It's in the joy of my friend Rick, who just became a grandfather, and tells me that having a grandchild slows you way down, because you have to adjust to Baby Time. And babies don't do hurry. . . . It's around the table in a little breakfast room on Brendenwood Terrace that time cannot erase from my mind."

BIBLE CONNECT

Work through some of these questions with your group, but don't feel pressured to talk about them all. Finish any questions you don't get to in your individual time later in the week. If you are short on time, focus on questions 1, 3, 6-9.

1. As we consider what it means to move away from the table and out to serve in the world, let's look at the life of a woman named Dorcas. We don't know a lot about Dorcas herself, but what we do know can be found in Acts 9—the same chapter in the Bible in which Paul's conversion experience is recorded, so Dorcas is in good company. Read Acts 9:36-43 and jot down or talk about all the facts you can gather about Dorcas—what was she known for, where did she live, who were her friends, what happened to her, etc.

2. What can you guess about Dorcas since you know how much she was able to do for others while she was alive, and how her body was treated after she died? Who cried for Dorcas?

3. Have three members of your group each read one of these sets of verses, all from Acts 9: a) verses 1a, 22, and 31; b) verses 32-35; c) verses 37, 40, and 42. Talk about the similarities and differences in these three stories of transformation. What did it take in each for change to occur? What was the effect?

4. Read Romans 12:1-5. What kind of sacrifice must you make to experience transformation? What kind of effect could your transformation have on the family of believers? How have you been affected by the transformation of others?

5. Read James 1:27. What is the religion that is considered pure? Why do you think James pairs the two ideas of serving others and not being polluted by the world? Read on in James 2:1-17. What in those verses might tell us what James considered as being "pollution"? What else do we learn about his thoughts on serving others?

6. For the rest of our study, we'll turn from thinking about how we can connect with and serve others to thinking about how we can connect with and serve Jesus. In Chapter 14 of *I'd Like You More*, John Ortberg refers to the Bible as a love story—a story of God's love for his people. And at the heart of that story lies the key to the mystery of intimacy. The story begins with God's searching in the garden ("Where are you?"), and it culminates in Jesus' great submission in the garden ("Not as I will, but as you will"), and the resurrection that came three days later. Though we in our humanness separated ourselves from God, God became fully human to bring us back together—to share in our experience. Let's look at some of the human moments in Jesus' life, beginning with Luke 2. Read verses 1-7, 21-24, 42-48, and 51. Consider what aspects of the experiences in those verses are like any human's experience (share your own stories too), and what aspects are different from our own life experiences.

7. Let's continue considering Jesus' life experiences. Read these verses from the beginning of his ministry in Luke 4:1, 2, 16, 22-30 and in Luke 5:15, 16. What about these

experiences stands out to you? What reminds you of experiences you have had?

8. Consider these emotional experiences of Jesus: when he was surprised—Luke 7:9; when he was moved—verses 12, 13; when he was annoyed by criticism—verses 33, 34; when he was fed up—9:41; when he was fired up—12:49-51; when he was snappy—13:31-33; when he was grieved—19:41-44; when he was in anguish—22:44. Can you relate to these experiences? What does it mean to you to know that Jesus had these emotions?

9. Consider these physical and social experiences of Jesus: when he was tired—John 4:6; when his mom embarrassed him—John 2:4; when he needed some time on his own—Matthew 14:13, 22, 23; when his mouth got him into hot water—John 8:58, 59 and John 10:31-33; when some of his fans left him—John 6:66; when he was betrayed by a friend—Matthew 26:47-50; when he was hurt and humiliated—Luke 22:63-65, John 18:22, 19:1-3; when his body was taken and buried—Luke 23:53, John 19:38-42. What do you learn about Jesus from these experiences? What does it mean to you to know Jesus went through these things?

GO OUT

-   Pray together.
-   Talk about where you can meet together to perform your act of service.

- Discuss next steps (your next study material, where people can go to learn and grow more as disciples, etc.).
- Use the space below to jot down a couple thoughts you want to remember.

_____

_____

_____

_____

OUT OF GROUP

PRAY

As you conclude this study, commit to staying in communication with God. Look back in your notes and remember any exercises you tried that worked for you (or ones you haven't tried yet). Put reminders in your phone or on your calendar to try those exercises again. It takes a while to adopt new good habits, or to change old bad ones. Use technology to your advantage. A simple alarm set to remind you to greet someone every day could be the thing that helps you stay on the path to developing deeper connections. Keep the conversation about your fears going between you and God. Keep bringing to Jesus your feelings about the people in your life and the experiences you've had with them. And continue to ask God to show you opportunities to get closer to others.

Slightly Awkward Exercise 1

Fill in this simple chart on the next page. Consider your regular weekly activities. Shade in the boxes that represent times when you feel most "with it"—when your mind is sharp, when you have energy, or when you are fully involved in what you are doing. Use the darkest shading for the times you feel at your best, lighter shading for times when you are not so engaged (or when you are tired, zoning out, etc.), and leave boxes completely blank when you are asleep or otherwise completely disengaged.

When you have finished filling in the chart, look back over the way you've shaded it and consider this: In the darkest times, the times you are at your best—who is with you? Who is getting to share in the best of you? And in your lighter times, who is with you then? Who consistently gets to share in the times when you are least alert and engaged? At which times are you most likely to be communicating with God?

· · · · · · · · · ·

	SUN	MON	TUE	WED	THU	FRI	SAT
4-5am							
6-7							
7-8							
8-9							
9-10							
10-11							
11-12pm							
12-1							
1-2							
2-3							
3-4							
4-5							
5-6							
6-7							
7-8							
8-9							
9-10							
10-11							
11-12am							
12-1							
1-2							
2-3							
3-4							

CONNECT AGAIN

Go back and think through the things you did and talked about with your group. Reflect on these things and write about your impressions.

What's something new you learned about the people in your group?

_____

_____

_____

_____

_____

What's something you learned or revisited about yourself?

_____

_____

_____

_____

_____

What is one new thing you learned about intimacy or connecting with others during the time with your group?

_____

_____

_____

_____

Think about the idea that "*intimacy* without *outimacy* leads to stagnation and death." Do you agree or disagree with this statement? What does the idea of outimacy mean to you? What relationships do you have now that could benefit from some outimacy?

_____

_____

_____

_____

Slightly Awkward Exercise 2

At his last gathering around a table with his friends, before he was arrested, Jesus did something unusual. He washed their dirty feet (John 13:1-17). There are a couple of interesting things about this act. One is that Jesus could have served his friends in any way—he could have brought them food, he could have fetched water, he could have made them comfortable with pillows, he could have simply placed a basin of water out for them to wash themselves. He could have done many things, but he chose the lowliest thing. He chose the dirtiest chore, and the one considered perhaps most unlikely for a rabbi to perform—to be so intimately associated with a part of the body that is still considered vulgar in much of the world (particularly in some Asian and Middle Eastern cultures).

The second thing to note is that this exercise required audience participation—the disciples had to submit to being washed. Peter tried to refuse Jesus, in fact, but Jesus said that Peter would "have no part" with Jesus unless he allowed his feet to be washed. The men had to let their Lord see the dirt on them and wipe it away.

For this exercise, seek to do the lowliest thing. Do the least thing you can do for someone else. And let someone else do the least for you. What is the one chore at your workplace that no one wants to do? Do that. What is the one thing in your house that everyone wants to pass off onto someone else? Do that. Change the diapers, pick up the dog poo, clean the toilet, take out the trash. Do the least thing. Then let someone help you with your lowliest task. And remember, sometimes those lowly things don't involve any kind of dirt you can see—more often than not, the nitty-gritty stuff of life comes in the form of emotional and social interactions. Drive someone to get a dreaded test done, go with a friend to an AA meeting, encourage a student before a final exam, be willing to accompany a person to her high school reunion.

Ask these questions of the people in your life: "What's the hardest thing you have on your plate this week? What's the thing you are most often dreading?" When you've got answers, figure out how to help them with those things.

Then ask yourself the same questions. When you've got answers, reach out and ask some people to help you with your lowly things. Don't fret about the dirt they might see—let them see the dirt of your life and help to wipe it away.

. . . .

What about serving others is easy for you? What about serving others is hard? What experiences have you had with serving others as part of a group?

_____

_____

_____

_____

_____

Read through the Bible verses that you talked about with your group. Be sure also to read through any that you didn't have time to discuss in the group. What did you think about the stories of transformation from Acts 9? Have you ever been personally affected by someone's service or generosity? How did being on the receiving end of that change you?

_____

_____

_____

_____

Consider the experiences of Jesus that were discussed in the Bible study questions. Think of one experience Jesus had that you can easily relate to. Why do you relate to that experience so well?

_____

_____

_____

Complete this sentence: When I think about how Jesus _____
_____, I feel closer to him.

_____

_____

_____

_____

Consider one experience Jesus had while he was living on this earth
that you find difficult to understand. What makes it so hard for you
to relate to that experience?

_____

_____

_____

_____

Complete this sentence: I'd like to understand more about how Jesus

_____

_____

_____

_____

Ortberg began talking about our relationship with God by looking
at the story of God and the first humans. He said God came to walk
in the garden and put out the "simplest bid for intimate connection,
repeated by every human being who ever lived: 'Want to go for a
walk?'" The man and woman then did not want to—or maybe they
did, but felt they were too ashamed to say so. What about you? Do
you want to go for a walk? Do you want to go for a walk with God?

What would you like to say to him? What subjects would you be hoping he might cover? Imagine how that conversation might go and write it out here.

_____

_____

_____

_____

Slightly Awkward Exercise 3

The subtitle of Ortberg's book—the book this study has been based on—is *Getting Real about Getting Close*. But it could have also been *Getting Closer to Being Real*. In the last chapter of the book, Ortberg talks about what real intimacy looks like, and how Jesus lived that out as an example for us. Ortberg gives some specific examples of ways he would like to be more real:

- To own my own story
- To understand my own worth
- To let go of other's opinions of me
- To be healed of everything that makes me want to hide: greed, lust, judging, deceit, pettiness, envy
- To be genuine—so that what you see is what you get

What would you add to this list? Write below your own wish list for being real:

_____

_____

_____

_____

Think of one step you can take this week toward being more real with God, and more real with others. Practice taking that step every day and push yourself to do more.

· · · · · · · · · ·

Before you leave this study, go back to the first session and find the intimacy quotient surveys you took about your intimacy levels with others and with God. Go through those statements and questions again and see if any of your answers have changed. If they haven't, spend some time thinking about why that is, and what you need to do to improve your connections with others. What do you need to do to get closer to God?

PRAY

Pray this prayer based on 1 John 4:10:

God, I am drawn to love you because you are so good. And when you do good things for me, I feel that love even more. But I want to love like you do. To love others not for what they can do, but to love no matter what—in good times and bad, in the times when things are easy and free and in the times when things are messy and tangled. I want to share in the experiences of others in a way that creates connection. I want to know Jesus better, so I can see what real human life looks like, and follow his example. I want to be real—with you, with my loved ones, with anyone. Thank you for sending your Son to us; for letting him sacrifice his perfect, pure, unburdened life to take on our messy, hard, and tangled days. Thank you for his love that makes us able to become real, for always. Amen.

GET REAL

As you leave this study

- Think of someone who might like to share your copy of *I'd Like You More*. If you don't have a copy yet, consider getting one and reading it.

- Be aware of how you are spending your time this week and who you are spending it with.

- Consider ways you can do one of the "lowly things" for someone in the coming weeks.

- Send your group members personal thank-you notes or texts to thank them for their participation in the group.

- If you won't be meeting with this particular group any-more, talk with your fellow group members to see how you can stay connected. If you will be continuing to meet together, discuss what will be the next subject you will focus on. Check out the pages in the back of this book to find some information on other useful resources or go to www.davidccook.com

- Think about this big statement: "Intimacy with God isn't mostly something I *do*, but something I receive."

LEADER PREP

Take some time to reflect on this study and jot down your thoughts:

What are some things I want to remember about leading this study?

_____

_____

_____

_____

What things were brought up that I'd like to address more, either with others or in my own personal study time?

_____

_____

_____

_____

What special prayer needs does the group have that I can continue to pray about?

_____

_____

_____

_____

What Bible passages from this study have stuck with me?

_____

_____

_____

_____

_____

What questions do I have about relationships that I need to explore more?

_____

_____

_____

_____

_____

What am I really challenged to do now?

_____

_____

_____

_____

_____

Who do I need to get real with or get closer to today?

_____

_____

_____

_____

NOTES

NOTES

NOTES

NOTES

NOTES

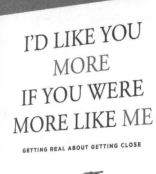

Journey with Your Church through the Bible's 40 Biggest Ideas

Are you looking to increase Bible engagement at your church? This 8-week church-wide program opens up the whole Bible to those who read Scripture regularly, as well as those who are just beginning. *The Good Book Church Campaign Kit* explores 40 key Bible chapters that lay the foundation for understanding the entirety of Scripture. As your church learns more about the Bible's biggest ideas, you will be prepared to step out into the world to offer joy, peace, and hope to your community.

Deron Spoo is the pastor of First Baptist Church in Tulsa, Oklahoma. Over the past 16 years, Spoo has guided the church as it transitions from being simply a downtown church to a regional church committed to urban ministry. His television devotionals, *First Things First*, reach 100,000 people each week. Spoo is a graduate of Southwestern Baptist Theological Seminary. He and his wife, Paula, have three children.